PRAISE FOR *I WISH YOU TRIPLETS*

"What a fantastic book... like reading a mystery, racing to see what happens ... and then finding clarity and the triumph of the ending. It was an extraordinary experience... I've never felt quite this way before with any book."

> — Abigail Thomas, *New York Times* bestselling author of *A Three Dog Life*

"DeLuca's memoir blends brilliance, raw emotion, humor, and extraordinary insight, examining with crystalline honesty how a spouse can blindside a profoundly loving and committed partner. Her willingness to dig through 'his and hers' sins of omission and commission and the family history underlying actions that set the scene for disaster provides a remarkably candid read. DeLuca cuts through the layers of longing and grief to find truth and comfort, gifting the reader with the most satisfying of reads, providing both page-turning 'gotta know' and deeply rewarding conclusions."

> — Randy Susan Meyers, international bestselling author of *WAISTED*

"DeLuca's memoir is gripping and emotionally stirring as it weaves together grief, laughter, outrage, and redemption. She speaks directly about the shock and upheaval of betrayal, of what it means to confront change at a stage of life when we often expect complacency. DeLuca is a master clinician at work on herself, charging fearlessly down the path of making sense of it all. There are no simple villains and victims here, but full people. Her rare combination of beautiful writing, cool mindedness and warm loving heart make for a deep meditation on humanity from which you emerge changed."

> — Orna Guralnik, psychologist, psychoanalyst and star of hit Showtime series Couples Therapy

"I love *If You Must Go, I Wish you Triplets!* Reading Ginny Deluca is like sitting across from your funniest, wisest friend over coffee. Her story of late life love and loss is layered and rich, and endlessly interesting. Deluca got me to think more deeply about my relationships, about how we make space for each other's hurts, and how to best tend to our own."

— Alysia Abbott, writer, teacher, speaker, and author of the
acclaimed memoir *FAIRYLAND: A Memoir of My Father*

"Ginny DeLuca takes us through the terrain of love and loss in middle-age with grace, incredible humor and insight. I had so much fun reading it. I could not put this book down. I was desperate to know what happened to the heroine. Buy one for yourself, and another one for your best friend."

— Sarah Ruhl, two-time Pulitzer Prize finalist, playwright, author of
the memoir, *Smile*

"This intimate, vulnerable memoir is an absolute pleasure to read, by turns hilarious, frank, and full of wisdom, making it difficult to put down. Readers will love Virgina DeLuca's voice and the central lesson of her story: When we think we're searching for answers from others, we're really searching for ourselves."

— Maya Shanbhag Lang, author of acclaimed memoir of *What We
Carry*

"If You Must Go, I Wish You Triplets is a testament to the vital force that is radical self-love, particularly later in life. With a psychotherapist's attention, and in compassionate, deeply moving and evocative prose, Virginia DeLuca examines the loss and *grief-land* a woman in her sixties must navigate after her husband leaves. What she finds is that loving fearlessly, no matter how the story ends, is the only thing worth planning in life. This is a beautiful book that speaks to us all, a poignant exploration of family and self-love full of humor, truth, and tenderness."

— Ani Gjika, award winning poet, and literary translator, and the
author of the memoir *An Unruled, Body,* winner of Restless
Books' 2021 Prize

"This book stacks losses like stone in a seaside sculpture—making beautiful what would otherwise be plain and simply hardened. Through a painful narrative of betrayal and backstory, Virgina DeLuca shows us that second chances can be worth it, even if they end up requiring a third act. I would recommend this book to anyone who might need the reminder that on the other side of today: is tomorrow; and until then: we have rom-coms to help us pass the time."

— Theresa Okokon, award-winning writer, storyteller, and teacher.
Her first book is the essay collection *Who I Always Was*

"As you travel with Ginny through grief-land, you'll laugh, you'll cry, you'll undoubtedly want to punch her husband, but most of all, you'll learn how to overcome the unthinkable with grace and purpose. A therapist's hilarious, yet wise perspective and must-read for anyone navigating betrayal."

— **Karen Kirsten, international seller of** *Irena's Gift: An Epic WWII Memoir of Sisters, Secrets, and Survival*

"If You Must Go, I Wish You Triplets is one of the most honest, raw, and satisfying memoirs I have read. In a voice that invites the reader in close and never falters, Virginia Deluca, a therapist who believes she should have known better, creates a stunning memoir about the shock of betrayal and divorce during her sixties. Deluca's fierce self-searching, humor, and willingness to share the roller coaster ride left me breathless, grateful for every page."

— **Linda Katherine, author of** *Memory Slips, A is for Always*, **and the forthcoming** *Black Angel*

If You Must Go, I Wish You Triplets

If You Must Go, I Wish You Triplets

A Memoir

Virginia DeLuca

Apprentice
House Press
Loyola University Maryland

Library of Congress Control Number: 2025931864

First Edition

Casebound ISBN: 978-1-62720-554-2
Paperback ISBN: 978-1-62720-555-9
Ebook ISBN: 978-1-62720-556-6

Cover by Niki Ignacio
Edited by Sophia Strocko
Internal Design by Niki Ignacio
Editorial Development by Aspen Shelton
Promotional Development by Maggie O'Donnell

Published by Apprentice House Press

Apprentice
House Press
Loyola University Maryland

Loyola University Maryland
4501 N. Charles Street, Baltimore, MD 21210
410.617.5265
www.ApprenticeHouse.com
info@ApprenticeHouse.com

Also by Virginia DeLuca

As If Women Mattered

For my grandchildren: Darwin, Brighid, Forest, Sylvie, Oakley, Luca, and Hazel.

And for my brothers' grandchildren: Michael, Silas, Sydney, Cole, Isabella, John Joseph, Leif, and Heyward

Remember to love fearlessly.

AUTHOR'S NOTE

Writing a memoir involves assembling imperfect and subjective memories. To tell my story, I relied on my notes, emails, texts, and journals to detail the events whenever possible. I know others have different perspectives on this story, and I take full responsibility for my version. As requested, I changed a few names and identifying information to protect privacy. My family members have given me permission for them to be included and identified in this book.

Short excerpts of this work have appeared, in slightly different form, in *The Iowa Review, The Writer Magazine, and The Huffington Post.*

PROLOGUE

Sexy. Whenever I think of Perry and how we were, I think sexy. The thought makes me smile—a buoyant inner smile, almost smug. Falling in love at forty-seven and marrying at fifty-two is both phenomenal and frightening. But then again, falling in love is always phenomenal and frightening.

However, in your fifties, the relationship comes with an end date built-in.

Oh, I know some people claim that fifty is the new thirty and all that. But for me, when Perry and I married, I was keenly aware that one of us would have to usher the other out. Maybe not for another thirty years or so, knock on wood, but Perry's parents both died in their early sixties. I'd buried many loved ones already. I just wanted it to be Perry ushering me out.

I should have remembered: *Be careful what you wish for.*

***

Before meeting Perry, I'd go about my day, striding between work meetings and appointments, feeling dumpy. In flats with knee-length skirts and suit jackets, I felt ... well, old. After meeting Perry, I strode in those same flat shoes with my soft belly, my fleshy hips, and my upper arms jiggling, and I felt ... well, sexy. Even my brown curls bounced.

Of course, nothing about my body had changed, but I felt altogether different. The openness of our desire, the undeniable fact of it, was a gift. I'd never before felt that way. Ever. Not at thirteen, when my junior high school boyfriend kissed me, and I was so busy redirecting his wandering hands, I experienced nothing but awkwardness. Not when my childhood friend Judy and I explored each other's bodies with an exciting but tentative interest. And not with my first husband, Dan, a relationship that lasted long past its expiration date.

I wasn't just enamored with Perry, I was captivated by who I became while with him: sensual, adventurous, brave.

When we first met, Perry was tan from playing tennis. Dark forearms and neck. He had pale blue eyes with deep laugh lines and gray hair just beginning to tinge his brown hair. Barrel-chested with thighs like tree trunks, he was five foot ten to my five foot five. We fit well together.

Perry taught English as a Second Language in New Hampshire. Kids in their early teens arrived from all parts of the world speaking no English. Perry exuded calm. Complemented by kind eyes, his smile said *everything would be okay*.

I was a psychotherapist, and like Perry, I was skilled at soothing people in crisis, helping them recognize they had the strength to deal with whatever life hurled at them. I also had recently launched my three twenty-something sons into the world. Free for the first time in decades from the daily responsibilities of caring for children, I was giddy with possibilities.

***

Over the years, Perry and I developed an easy rhythm. Our routines, both prosaic and sublime, delighted me. We spent entire weekend afternoons exploring the local library and drinking coffee at Breaking New Grounds, in Portsmouth, New Hampshire. We walked the beaches of Maine and sketched the rocks at low tide. We cooked together, nothing fancy, eating copious amounts of broccoli and broiled chicken, relishing and feeling virtuous in our healthful simplicity. Occasionally, we ate popcorn for dinner as we read books by the fire.

We took care of each other, inconsequential things: me placing a water glass on his bedside table, him refilling my coffee as I wrote in the morning. Perry was attentive. When texting became part of our lives, there were little check-ins throughout the day:

> *Drive carefully on the way home, huge thunderstorm*
> *expected*
> Or:
> *Delicious dinner ready, don't eat junk food* ☺

We happily shared our world, expansive with our love. Perry's sister and brothers and their families joined my family as we hiked the coastal routes of Maine and ate Thanksgiving turkey together. Friends drove up from Boston. We hosted parties for his current and former students and their families.

Through the years, my kids and their various significant others stayed with us for weekends, joined us for holidays. We danced at their weddings, and when their babies began arriving, we would bring them to the ocean.

We touched each other often, like shorthand. *I'm here. I'm here.* He wasn't a big talker, and that was fine. The touch, I thought, does not lie.

CHAPTER 1

I say goodbye to my last client of the day and check my phone, expecting the usual text from Perry about dinner. Maybe even a suggestion of meeting up at Three Chimneys Inn for drinks to watch the May sun slant over the Oyster River.

> *I won't be there when you get home. Had a bad day.*
> *Need time alone.*

Perry's always home from teaching by the time I arrive on Wednesdays. Something at work must have seriously upset him.

When I call to check, I'm sent right to voicemail. I leave a message murmuring love and saying I hope it's nothing too awful. Then I pack up my computer bag, some files, and purse and head down the lifeless gray-green corridor common to every probation office. As if being on probation isn't depressing enough, we subject clients to the most disheartening colors possible.

I lead community therapy groups for violent offenders in a small town in Maine, helping men break patterns of abuse and assault. After doing this work for over twenty years, I remain astounded at the power of these groups to effect change. Severely wounded people possess a tremendous capacity to hurt others. However, I learned that they can develop the ability to recognize those hurts and alter their behaviors. It is difficult and draining work for everyone, and today's been a long day.

I tell the probation officer in charge that I'm finished and wait with her to lock up and walk out together. She is funny, wears a gun slung on her hip, and loves to gossip. We've become friends. Typically, we would banter in the parking lot, but I'm eager to get home. If the light holds, Perry and I can walk along the Oyster River, half a mile from our house. I want nothing more than to shake off the institutional paint color and the weight of other people's troubles. I anticipate with pleasure the feel of Perry's hand in mine as we stroll.

I handle a few work calls on my way home from Biddeford, Maine. Since I'm the director of treatment, clinicians often call me at the end of the day with questions or concerns about clients. Working with violent offenders means always being on alert. One client is about to be released from probation, but he disclosed another assault he's never been charged with. Another was absent from the group for two weeks and isn't answering his phone. A third left the state to attend a relative's birthday party without informing his probation officer. Situations that once unnerved me are at least familiar now, but still, they raise all our anxieties.

In between these conversations, I try Perry again. He does not pick up, and I begin to worry. It's not like him to ignore my calls.

The drive home is long but beautiful. I like to take the route down the coast from Maine to New Hampshire, passing through Wells, Kennebunk, Ogunquit, York, and Kittery, where I glimpse the ocean and the gulls diving for fish in the marshes. These small seaside towns burst into crowded resorts in summer, but in the off-season, they resemble the small fishing villages they once were. Reaching the bridge over the Piscataqua River, which separates Maine and New Hampshire, I catch sight of the church steeple in Market Square. I head west and drive over the bay into Durham, a sleepy town filled with coffee shops, copy stores, and pizza joints serving the University of New Hampshire students.

Our house is three levels built into the top of a hill, surrounded by woods, not far from the campus. I wind my car up the steep drive fringed with yellow forsythia and deep purple azaleas.

As warned, Perry's vehicle is not in its usual spot by the garage. I check my phone. No messages. I call. Again, it goes directly to voicemail. Queasy, I tell myself there is nothing to worry about.

I drop my computer bag and tote inside the house and change into sweats.

I call again. Where is he?

Darkness descends. Impossible to think or sit still, I flip on the lights and pace between the kitchen and the couch. I work with people whose lives went horribly off the rails because of impulsive, unthought-out choices they made, so it's no surprise I begin to play out worst-case scenarios. My workdays are filled with clients trying to explain what was going on when they made those disastrous split-second decisions that seemed reasonable. Many of their stories begin with, "So, I was having a really bad day at work" or "I had a terrible fight with my girlfriend."

Now it's ten o'clock—five hours since his text. I leave voice messages: *I'm worried. What's wrong?* I text the same. *Let me know if you're all right.* Perry is never out of touch for this long.

Finally, an email comes. Not a phone call. Not a text. This is very odd behavior.

> Subject line: Talking
> *Gin,*
> *I am safe and okay—I drank a few beers after work*
> *and don't want to drive, so I found a motel in Dover.*
> *I will stay in tonight.*

Dover is only the next town over. How many beers did he have? Perry's not a regular drinker. Why wouldn't he simply ask me to pick him up?

I read more.

I held in my worries about things. I started worrying
I'd end up with a stroke or heart attack if we didn't
talk soon. I've been a mess as far as communicating
any of this goes, and I apologize for that.
Perry

I stare at the words on the screen. He held in his worries about
what things? He'd end up with a heart attack if we didn't talk
about *what*, exactly? I study these sentences for a long time, trying
to understand what on earth he's attempting to communicate.

I call to offer to go to the motel and drive him home. Again, he
does not pick up. I leave a message. Little do I know how familiar
this is going to become.

I send an email: *Sweetie, what's happened?*

He emails back:

I'm sorry for not answering the phone, but I don't
want to talk tonight. I do want us to talk later. I
couldn't find it in me to start now, sitting together in
person.

I blink at his message, wondering why we are emailing and not
talking. I'm wondering why my husband is not replying to texts
and calls and why, even though he is one town over, he does not
want to come home.

CHAPTER 2

Somehow that night, I fall asleep. An ominous feeling of dread wakes me from a deep sleep, and I'm jolted into full alert. It's before dawn, and I'm still on the couch, still clutching my cell phone. When I open my phone, a series of emails from Perry greets me, each one a separate sentence.

SUBJECT LINE: Thoughts
Things changed for me since coming back from my
trip to Vietnam.

A few months ago, Perry traveled to Vietnam over Christmas break to teach English. For years, he dreamed of teaching overseas. A former student intern arranged for him to be a guest teacher at a university in Da Nang. When he returned, exuberant, I was thrilled he had fulfilled a lifelong ambition. We'd always been eager to support one another's dreams. Cuddled on the couch, we watched the videos he made of teaching adult students and scrolled through his endless photographs of fishermen working on the beach at dawn.

I had chosen not to join him on this trip. Instead, I'd planned to use the holiday break to finish revisions on the novel I was submitting to a contest. The winner would be published. It was a long shot, but I was determined to try. Miracles can happen.

My novel began years ago, lifetimes ago, written in fits and spurts on the edges of my life. I lugged unopened boxes of drafts from house to house each time I moved. Once, when packing, I almost tossed them all out, but at the last minute, I wrote *Attic* on the cartons.

Living with Perry had created enough calm and peace for me to pull the boxes out of hiding and begin again. While Perry was off realizing his dream, I had the space to concentrate, fulfilling mine. I spread my pages on the living room floor and worked in the pure luxury of uninterrupted time for a solid week.

I turn to the next email.

> *The sweetness and intimacy of sharing life with you are very real, including the warmth of supporting you in the love you give your kids and extended family and now the grandkids.*

I frown. He obviously thinks he is telling me something, but I have no idea what. Obliqueness isn't his style, though he's not a person who shares every thought. Words don't tumble out of his mouth, falling over each other, as mine tend to do. If upset, he'll go for a walk, return home, and calmly tell me what's bothering him in complete, unjumbled sentences. I lean toward the opposite. When upset, I blurt out what's on my mind, admittedly a bit disjointedly. Afterward, I go off to sit by the Oyster River while I sort out what I'm feeling.

I open the following email.

> *I don't think it's enough for me to be happy and fulfilled.*

Fear, immediate and physical, lands in my solar plexus, making it difficult to breathe. My mind skitters like a rock skimming over a calm ocean. There is nothing to be afraid of, I tell myself. These past months, we've been talking about downsizing and moving to Boston to be closer to my kids and grandkids. Is he trying to tell me he doesn't want to do this? That's fine. I take deep breaths, hoping to release clenched muscles. We can figure out a different plan. I turn to the next message.

I find myself wanting to make a family of my own, even at this advanced age.

What?
I push off the couch. I need to move. I wash my face and make coffee. Working fiercely to shift into denial, I don't read the following email. Trained therapist Ginny sees the signs, observing me at a distance. I'm determined to keep awareness at bay with frantic busyness.

But I know better. Clutching my coffee, I sink to the couch.

I want to talk and, somehow if it's possible, to keep our closeness... I'm wondering if after you tell me to go F myself whether we can talk. I think I know what I'm doing, but in any case, I needed to find a way to get out what I started holding inside. I'm sorry it was in this hurtful way.

I try to absorb the words. I am incredulous. *I think I know what I'm doing.* What is it that you're doing? I want to ask him. What is it, precisely, that you've been holding on to for so long?

In any communication, there is always a gap between the speaker and the listener. In long partnerships, it's common for one person to be caught off guard by the previously unspoken (or unheard) feelings of the other. In my therapy practice, I often help couples as one member struggles with shocking information they were not prepared for.

That person is now me.

I grip my mug, needing to hold on tightly to something. The inability to grasp my situation makes me woozy.

But conceivably, Perry is merely trying to start a conversation, even if he's going about it in a bizarre and hurtful way. Perhaps my job right now is to keep the conversation going. This I can live with. So often, I see couples shut down because one person feels hurt. At work, I quote a favorite line from Alain de Botton: "The emotionally intelligent person knows that they will only ever be mentally healthy in a few areas and at certain moments, but is committed to fathoming their inadequacies and warning others of them in good time, with apology and charm."

In other words, we all have pockets of crazy.

Is Perry ending our fourteen-year relationship via email?

To make babies?

The prospect of this seems utterly ridiculous. Perry is sixty.

No. This must be Perry encountering his own pocket of crazy.

I reread the emails compulsively. I feel like a detective trying to sleuth out their meaning. I picture Perry in some motel room in Dover. I imagine him pacing the grungy carpet or stretched out on a bed with a scratchy covering.

This time, when I call, he picks up.

"You need to come home." I don't bother with hello.

"But I'm at school."

"You're at *work*?" I'm baffled. Here I am, imagining him in crisis, sitting slumped, hungover, and dejected in a cheap motel, and he's going about his day. I can't tell if I'm angry or relieved.

Typically, on Thursdays, I drive to Cambridge to treat clients in my private practice. I stay over, often visiting friends. On Fridays, I take care of my grandkids. This is my weekly routine, the rhythm of my circuit: New Hampshire to Maine early in the week, then down to Boston at the end of it. Today, I cancel my appointments and beg off grandparent duty. I don't tell anyone what happened. I don't know what to say.

I pace. I take a shower. I lie on the couch. I try to read a magazine.

Perry arrives an hour later.

"What's happening?" I ask with an edge of panic.

He appears okay. He's dressed in his school clothes—a sports shirt and chinos. I can smell the Irish Spring soap he likes. Does he carry a bar of it in his school bag? Did he *plan* on spending the night at the motel? I can't imagine what I must look like after a night curled on the couch. All I know is that he seems perfectly fine, while I feel agitated, unsteady, and shaky.

He sits down across from me. "I want a divorce," he announces without preamble. "I'm not attracted to you anymore. I want children of my own." His words rush out as though he's rehearsed the lines, afraid he'd forget one.

"What?" I sit up. I can't make sense of his sounds. It's as though he's speaking in a foreign language. Is this how his students feel—shocked by the words coming at them too fast?

He continues to talk, stammering in a rush. I catch phrases and snippets: *just realized ... last chance ...* He is babbling.

When faced with disaster, I become hyperfocused, with excellent diction. In times of crisis, I exhibit supernatural calm. All emotions of fear, sadness, and hysteria vanish. Cold assessment predominates. I'm the person you want around when a kid cracks his head open on the radiator and blood spurts everywhere. It's the skill of dissociation, learned early in childhood and, if employed judiciously, very handy.

But walk up behind me in a quiet room and say, "Hi," and my response might be a shriek. My startle reflex is extreme. Put me in a playground, and I fretfully visualize children falling off the slide or tumbling from the swings.

All morning, I've battled the anxious dread of picturing a toddler plummeting from an extreme height.

I study Perry, the man I love beyond reason and whom I trust with my most intimate feelings and thoughts. My partner with whom I experience acceptance and love as never before in my sixty-one years. As I regard him, this man speaking about not finding me attractive, about wanting a divorce, I transform. Panic and fear slide away. A chilly calm takes over.

"Do you have a mother in mind for these children?" I ask.

"No." He pauses, then adds, almost conversationally, "But I want to be free to pursue someone. There was a guidance counselor last year I was attracted to. Nothing happened, and she's left the school district, but I want to call her." He hurries on. "You might notice a charge of three nights for a hotel this past weekend, but I couldn't find the nerve to tell you, so I didn't stay there."

This past weekend? My thoughts scroll back to the visit from my oldest son and daughter-in-law and my one-year-old granddaughter. We ate lobster in Portsmouth. We strolled by the water. It was blissful.

I stand, my body rigid. "Have a good life." I give a tiny wave.

"Do you mind if I grab a few things?" he asks sheepishly. "I ... need some stuff ... for the hotel." He seems visibly relieved there isn't more of a scene.

I stare at him while he goes into the bedroom.

Five minutes later, he walks out with his gym duffle. I sink to the sofa.

I hear him open his car door and picture him throwing in his bag. The door slams and the tires crunch down the drive.

And then only silence.

I want a divorce. I'm not attracted to you anymore.

With those sentences I feel every one of my sixty-one years. My hips widen, my breasts sag, my wrinkles deepen. Every internalized belief and vision of what it means to be an old, unwanted, irrelevant woman becomes who I am.

I pop off the couch. I need to leave the house. Immediately. I grab my keys and my wallet, throw on a sweater, and bolt.

In downtown Durham, I buy wine and a pack of Marlboro Lights. I haven't smoked in years, but nothing else will soothe me.

I come home and begin calling everyone I know.

"Perry asked for a divorce because he wants babies," I announce to friends, to my children, to colleagues. "At sixty."

I need to make this real. It doesn't feel real. I crack bad jokes.

"At least I won't be obliged to take care of him when he's a drooling old man."

I must sound exceptionally odd. My children invite me to come live with them. Friends invite me to stay with them. I decline. I keep calling people.

I open the wine.

I unwrap the cigarettes.

I do not cry.

"I am so disoriented," I say over and over to whoever is listening.

I thought I could read people, understand people. I am a goddamn therapist. Perry and I have been making plans. We've spent the past few months arranging to put the house on the market and slowing down on work so we can travel and enjoy adventures while we're still mobile.

Two weeks ago, we went to Ogunquit, Maine, to celebrate fourteen years together. Only two weeks ago, we held hands on the beach, kissing and laughing as the frigid water caught our feet, talking about what we wanted for our future. A few months earlier, we'd taken a long-delayed trip to Rome and Tuscany, strolling through olive groves and talking over candlelit dinners. Just yesterday morning, he suggested we change our cable package so we could watch the Red Sox this summer.

"Maybe he has a brain tumor," says a friend.

"He's having an affair," announces another.

"Clearly, it's a nervous breakdown."

"He's had an affair, *and* she's pregnant," one decides.

"Perhaps it's a urinary tract infection. You know, elderly people can have psychosis with UTIs."

This suggestion comes from a much younger friend who thinks of sixty as elderly. I forgive her.

"He's an asshole," a friend of forty years tells me.

But I don't believe that. Perry has never been an asshole. He's the most gentle, caring man I've ever known.

I wrap myself in blankets even though it's seventy degrees outside. I am shaking and unable to process what has happened.

I wonder how I could have missed this, not seen it coming—but I don't even know what *it* is. We joked for years about him being an internal processor and me being an external processor. Now that feels like an understatement of monumental proportions.

I frequently expound to friends on the wonders of later-in-life love. Perry and I had synergy. No matter what, we always fell in step with each other. We might have our grumpy moods, bad days, or minor disagreements, but we have learned how to handle them. We were adults who understood who we were. We'd gone through our growing pains, and we knew how to be together. This was what I believed. Turns out, it wasn't true.

CHAPTER 3

Perry calls the following day and tells me he wants to deal with business: bank accounts and the divvying up of possessions. This was his second night away from me. Two nights, I think, as I listen to him say he doesn't want his paycheck auto deposited into our joint account. Two nights, and he wants to go through our storage unit to claim his stuff. We'd just packed and moved those items into storage a few weeks ago to reduce clutter in preparation for listing the house for sale. He must have known at the time that he was planning to leave. He said not one word.

I am two nights into Perry's world, two nights into a separation process that he has been mulling over for some quantity of time I may never know. I want to pry open his skull and riffle through his brain. I need to know precisely when he began planning this. In my work, I have seen patients wrestle with feelings of powerlessness. I know all too well that calm, serenity, or peace won't—can't—come from external sources, and certainly, it won't come from Perry. Still, I want answers.

I force myself to focus on practical details. My mother taught me to finish my chores before I played, and it has been my coping style since I was a girl. This is a useful thing for mothers to teach. It ensures that chores will get done. But the adult list of tasks is never truly finished, which creates inner tension. I often feel guilty or negligent when I shouldn't: when I choose to walk in the woods instead of washing dishes, laugh with my children instead of vacuuming, or curl up with Perry instead of completing end-of-month reports. On the flip side, in times of despair, making lists and firing through them soothes me.

With a deep breath, I turn to the credit card statements. In one week, Perry has spent $1,000 on hotel rooms he didn't use as he fortified himself to leave. I call up the credit card companies and tell them I've lost the cards. This way, Perry can't keep using them. If Perry wants to handle business, that's fine. Business it is. When he comes, I'll hand him the credit card offers that always arrive in the mail. He can use his own goddamn credit.

I add up all our debt. I add up our bills. I add up our take-home pay. I make myself a budget, and while I'm at it, I make one for Perry too. I want to drive home to him that he doesn't have money to rent hotel rooms and that he needs to find a place to live.

I'm good at the paperwork of life. I might not like it, and I don't have orderly files or clean drawers, but I open the mail as it comes, toss the fliers into the recycle bin, and pay bills on time. Rarely do I put something into a pile to consider later.

Perry does not have this skill. Towering piles of papers cover his desk, and when they threaten to topple, he swipes them all into brown paper bags and stashes them under the desk. He has other strengths, like stopping after school to pick up fresh salmon and broccoli for dinner.

I have a moment of panic—partly about money but mainly about my future. I glance around. What if the house doesn't sell? Even if I could afford to live here alone, there is no way I can manage it by myself in the winter. The drive is so steep that the plow can't make it up the hill. It has to be hand shoveled, a job that requires both of us working together for hours. When snow is predicted, we park at the bottom of the hill. One year, it snowed so often that we lost the use of the drive entirely. I can't imagine handling a winter here on my own. My muscles ache just thinking about it. I feel frail, a word I'd never before used to describe myself.

At the same time, I can't imagine leaving. I'm happy here. It's one of the few places I've lived where I didn't spend time thinking, *If only I could knock down this wall or build a small addition, it would be perfect.*

The house is a hexagon. All six sides have floor-to-ceiling windows. The first floor has always been Perry's domain, with his recliner, bookshelves, desk, and television. The second level is the kitchen, living room, and bedroom, with the living room dominated by a brick chimney that extends through the loft.

We installed a wood stove in the fireplace after losing electricity and heat for two weeks during our first winter here. Sitting on the L-shaped couch with our feet touching, we would follow the family of cardinals in the hemlock outside, the snow falling, the fire crackling, and our books open. Perry was the one who would split and stack the wood.

Off the kitchen is a deck built around a huge granite boulder shaded by an ancient sycamore. A black bear cub stared at us from that rock during our first spring here. I always hope the cub, or one of its descendants, will return. But we learned it was necessary to take down the bird feeders in early April because if bears start hanging around human dwellings, they will be shot. Not fair, of course, but that's the reality. The deer have a run they use between our property and our neighbors'. During one severe spring rainstorm, the rivers flooded and our hilltop became a refuge for small animals seeking higher ground. A mother fox carried her kits up and we heard them crying through the night. I will miss them all.

Also, there is my private workspace and desk in the loft above the living room. From there, I can spot the pileated woodpecker and watch the surrounding trees flame in autumn. I love this home.

Though the plan was for us to sell, and the first viewings are scheduled, I never imagined leaving on my own. It feels like I'm being evicted.

And if the house does sell, I have no idea where I'll go.

I decide I'm not ready. I refuse to be rushed out. I call the real estate agent and tell her to cancel any viewings over this weekend. I don't tell her why

In the bedroom, I grab two boxes and throw in Perry's shirts, belts, ties, underwear, shorts, and pants, and dump them in the garage. Hopefully, they'll mildew.

"This can't be happening," I say to Ricky when she checks in. Diane calls. Susan calls. Roz calls. Nancy calls.

My oldest son, Orion, Skypes from England, where he is visiting his in-laws with his wife and daughter, and says, "I can't believe Perry would do this, Mom." My son's shock comforts me.

Zac, my middle son, calls to say he, his wife, Cynthia, and the babies will drive up for dinner.

My youngest son, Josh, tells me he will come up from New York over Memorial Day weekend.

Nieces and nephews call.

Work friends call.

I am grateful. Without these calls, I would shatter into a million fragments.

***

That afternoon, Perry arrives to deal with finances. When he reaches the living room, he is crying so hard he can't speak.

"What happened?" I ask, startled.

He shakes his head and takes his handkerchief out of his pocket to wipe his face.

I am not accustomed to seeing Perry cry. "Talk to me," I say gently. "This is all so sudden."

He shakes his head again.

"Please tell me what's happening with you," I beg.

"I can't," he chokes out. "Not now."

His tears soften me. *Oh, so he doesn't truly want to leave me; he doesn't want to end our marriage.* I'm convinced his crying means he's in some sort of trouble. Later, I will wince at this, but at that time, he was a person I deeply loved; he'd only been gone two days; and he was clearly in great distress. I just didn't know why.

Finally, he calms down. He refuses to talk about why he is so upset but agrees to talk business. I explain which bills he needs to transfer to his account—his car payments, his gym membership, and so forth. His summer paycheck comes in June, and I planned to use it to cover the house taxes. He will still need to help with that. I write it all out for him as we talk. I am manager and secretary all at once. I simply do not believe our marriage is ending. Obviously, we are in crisis, but is our marriage and our life together finished? That isn't possible. On the other hand, in case I'm wrong, I'm determined to protect myself financially. I've already been divorced once. I know how it can go.

Years later, I will wonder how my life might have been different had I initially said no when he asked for a divorce.

At the time, it never even occurred to me. Later, I read a *New York Times* Modern Love essay by a woman whose husband had an affair with a younger woman. The author refused to let it end the marriage. They lived happily ever after. That essay will haunt me for a long time

But in this moment, as we sit on the couch, I do not fight. I do not yell or scream. I make a list. I prepare for his exit. Is it pride? Self-respect? Outrage? Wisdom? As a therapist, I feel I should know the answers, but I am numb. We drive separate cars to the bank.

CHAPTER 4

Perry and I arrive at the bank. A young woman greets us cheerfully.

"We are getting separated and need to unlink our accounts," I announce.

"Oh, oh," she chirps in alarm, and leads us to her cubicle.

Perry starts crying again.

The woman tries to give Perry a moment by chattering about the beautiful weather, the slow computer, the troublesome printer. She casts Perry worried glances. She passes him tissues. He's sobbing so hard, he needs to leave the cubicle.

She throws me a look that says, *You bitch.*

I sigh. The man who hid his feelings so successfully that I never saw them coming couldn't hide them a bit longer? I mentally roll my eyes and silently curse him out as we wait for him to return.

Later, Perry calls. "I felt almost a physical tearing inside watching you leave the bank today." He's weeping again and can barely get the words out. "I still feel like calling you *hon* or *sweetie*."

When I hear this, many parts of me clamor for attention. The loudest declares: *See. Here's proof that he doesn't really want to leave.*

"Then why are you leaving?" I ask.

"I have to hang up now," he answers.

I fight the urge to throw the phone across the room in some dramatic out-of-the-movies gesture and instead drop it roughly on the couch. I want to roar in frustration. Why call me only to hang up? I'm absolutely certain that if I wanted to leave for some reason and finally did it, I'd be feeling relieved, even happy, at this point.

I don't imagine I'd tell him that I still feel like calling him *sweetie*.

Nothing about this makes sense.

***

The first time Perry called me *sweetie*, we were in his studio apartment in a converted mill in Dover, New Hampshire.

"Bathroom's free, sweetie."

We had been seeing each other for a month. What did *sweetie* mean in this context? I didn't know how to react to the word. This was my first foray into serious dating after an eighteen-year marriage, and terms of endearment hadn't been used in that relationship. I had no memory of my parents ever referring to each other affectionately. Perry had used the word so easily and readily that it stunned me.

As I washed my face, I created a whole world out of that word. He likes me, I thought, gazing at my reflection. He really likes me. Instantly, I pictured myself writing in a café in Paris (a place I'd never been) or hiking the Adirondacks, or merely perusing the bookstores with him months from now, and walking slush-covered sidewalks to read in a warm coffee shop. Anything was possible. At that moment, a world opened up for me that went beyond the roles of mother and therapist.

Gone immediately was the too-old-to-find-love woman.

I was now the adventurous having-a-love-affair woman.

I was the woman receiving a dozen long-stemmed roses and waking up in the Red Lion Inn.

I was sweetie and hon and babe.

***

After the disastrous visit to the bank, my son Zac and his family arrive from Boston with Chinese food for dinner. I play with the kids, watching six-month-old Forest try to crawl. Cynthia has told two-and-a-half-year-old Darwin that I am sad.

"Why are you sad, Nonna?"

"Because Grandpa doesn't want to live here with me anymore, and that makes me sad."

"I'll live with you," he says.

I laugh. It surprises me that I can. "Well, that makes me very happy."

It is calming to be with the kids—and exhausting. They leave, and I dissolve.

CHAPTER 5

Six weeks before Perry's announcement, on one of those cold gray March Saturdays that make New Englanders believe this is the year winter actually *won't* end, the publisher of the novel contest I'd entered left a message on my phone.

Perry and I had taken a walk around the neighborhood instead of beginning the job of sorting belongings and taking them to storage for our move. This was the kind of work Perry hated and kept putting off. I wanted to say *everyone hates packing, you are not that unique*, but I didn't. I merely reminded him that Joe, the handyman, was coming in the afternoon with his truck to take away the boxes and that the house was officially going on the market in a few weeks. We had to get this done. Perry did not share my sense of urgency about this chore, but he put an agreeable face on it.

Before we got down to work, I called back Tom Holbrook, the publisher. He congratulated me on winning first prize in the contest. The book would be published in the summer. He said they planned a reading for the launch at his Portsmouth store, RiverRun Bookstore, in late June. I gasped in such a way that Perry dropped the books he was carrying and hurried to my side. The publisher laughed at my reaction, saying it was a wonderful book, a great story, and well told. He said other nice things, but I was having a difficult time taking it all in.

When I got off the phone, my head was full of information that hadn't stuck: copy edit deadlines and cover designs and proofs.

"I did it!" I grinned at Perry. "Holy shit. My novel's getting published. Finally!"

My insides jumped all over the place, but I held still, believing if I moved too quickly, this dream would shatter.

I'd been writing all my life. I often joked that I thought with my fingers, not my brain, first using a pen, next a typewriter, and later a computer. Writing helped me know what I felt and believed. I even published a few things along the way. But I never seemed able to take myself seriously as a real writer.

When I was younger, I thought of writers as older individuals with more life experiences and certain of what they wanted to say. When I became older, writers were young people who understood that in order to dedicate themselves to the craft of writing, they shouldn't clutter up their lives with relationships and causes. Of course, both of those beliefs were untrue.

A month before Tom called, I turned sixty-one. For years and years, I had a sign from the writer Julie Cameron hanging over my desk.

"Do you know how old I'll be when I finally finish this thing?"
"Yes, the same age you'll be if you don't."

So, I kept going. Writing, reading books about writing, joining writing groups.

And now I was going to publish my novel. *As If Women Mattered* follows four women who met in the 1970s, a time when feminism was making front-page news. When I began the book, I never expected it to be a historical novel. I simply wanted to express the significance of the women's movement in my life.

That had been a heady time. In the 1950s, when I was a girl, our culture told us that women were emotional, weak, ditzy, and not interested in sex. Also, girls needed protection while being caretakers. We were told women were soft, quiet, not as smart as men, and too sensitive. And then, twenty years later, women all over the country were saying, "Oh, wait a goddamn minute. I will tell you who and what I am." All around me, women were uncovering, discovering, and recovering what being female meant. They were doing it loudly, messily, excitedly, and on a profoundly personal level. Recreating the definitions, woman by woman, until the very language was altered.

By the time my book was accepted for publication in 2014, much had changed in the world, but it turned out the struggles of my characters—the challenges of juggling work, motherhood, marriage or the judgments of remaining single; the acknowledgment of personal ambition; the ownership of our sexuality—were timeless.

I heard Perry talking to the handyman, Joe. Then Perry came to me, gave me an impressive kiss, and told me we would pack and move the stuff to storage tomorrow. Today, we were going to walk by the ocean and afterward celebrate at Café Med.

***

Perry's timing is atrocious. I know there never would've been a right time for him to leave, but there might have been better times. I randomly pull books from the bookshelf and toss them into an empty carton. What kind of person walks out on their sixty-one-year-old wife while selling a house without a thought or plan for how it will all get done? I consider why it even matters that I am sixty-one. Being dumped at any age sucks. But it does matter. *I'm not attracted to you anymore.* I'm old and now sexually unattractive.

Packing is arduous, dirty, physical work. And the emotions of leaving a beloved home are intense. Infinite decisions need to be made about what to keep, toss, or give away and to whom.

I empty another shelf. We built this life together. We built this home together. But for the dismantling and leaving, I'm on my own. The box is full, and I drag it behind the couch to be out of the way and begin to assemble another carton. Perry's lack of caring is so unfamiliar that I'm even more positive he's in some kind of trouble or having a mental breakdown. I remove a few more books.

Or maybe he has early-onset dementia?

This thought makes me stop throwing books. I sit at the table with a glass of water. Dementia would make sense, I think. His mother was completely debilitated from Parkinson's by this age. I grab my computer and immediately google early-onset dementia. According to the Alzheimer's Association, *very early dementia* may cause changes in personality and behavior—in ways that have nothing to do with memory loss.

I'm interrupted by a call from Tom confirming the date of the event next month to launch my book. I start pacing the length of the room, kicking the almost empty second box behind the couch. No more packing right now. No more indulging in the fantasy of dementia as the reason Perry wants to leave me. I have to focus on publishing.

***

"How am I going to get ready for the book launch?" I wail to Ricky, also a writer, when she calls.

"Don't worry. It's over six weeks away," she says calmly.

I, on the other hand, am not calm. This triumphant moment, the culmination of years of work, the fulfillment of my long-held dream, is eclipsed by the desolation of being tossed in the giveaway pile, too old to be of use. It freezes my brain and makes it impossible to think straight.

After Ricky and I say goodbye, I pour wine and take it out on the deck. I light a cigarette and listen to squirrels skittering through trees. They are loud. More than once while sitting on this deck, I've heard furious scurrying and imagined I'd spot a deer or a fox, but it's just a small gray squirrel.

I had visualized the launch event as a scene out of a movie. Perry would be in the front row beaming with pride, knowing it was our relationship, his love, that had given me the confidence and courage I needed to enter the contest. I imagined being surrounded by friends and family cheering for me.

Now, the launch feels irrelevant. I crush my cigarette out in a planter of begonias. Publication day is still momentous, I tell myself. The accomplishment is still great, but now it all feels like a chore, an unwanted obligation, something I must prepare for to get through.

The irony does not escape me. I'm so devastated by being left by a man that I can't focus on publishing a novel that celebrates women freeing themselves from being defined solely by their relationships with men. It's a humbling kind of humiliation. I laugh at the absurdity of it.

I go back inside, pour another glass of wine, and open my computer to try to choose what to read at the launch. Instead, I begin a new document titled *The Perry Leaving Journal.* It's only been three days, but it feels like a lifetime filled with a jumble of thoughts, reactions, and events I can't sort out.

I start creating a record, pasting in Perry's emails and texts. I transcribe our phone calls. Doing this calms me. This is the thing about writing. All the events in my life, devastating or exhilarating, can be put into words that force distance—at least for a moment—from the roiling emotions that threaten to drown me.

When I eventually climb into bed, hoping I'll be tired enough to sleep, I check my emails. There's one from my women's group: they are driving up from Boston tomorrow.

For decades, I belonged to a women's group. Back in the seventies, consciousness-raising groups like ours formed to discuss and explore all aspects of being female. Women telling the truth about their lives was a new and powerful tool for change. The personal was political.

Almost every week for over forty years, Ricky, Susan, Diane, and I have met at someone's house, put out a spread, and talked. Our group started when our children were babies. We were all working for an agency that counseled pregnant and postpartum women, and we decided to form our own support group. Ever since, we've talked through our various relationships, the deaths of family members, marital fights, divorces, and affairs. We exchanged books along with the minutiae of raising children. More recently, we've delved into the dramas of our adult children. We have shared everything from makeup tips to intense discussions about the state of the world and our ideas for fixing it all. So, of course, my group is here for me now.

I reach for a book on my nightstand. Peggy Orenstein's *Cinderella Ate My Daughter: Dispatches from the Front Lines of the New Girlie-Girl Culture.* The words on the page don't connect with each other. I close it and pick another one. *We Are All Completely Beside Ourselves* by Karen Joy Fowler. Again, the words don't penetrate my brain. These are books I would normally devour, that would keep me company. Reading has always anchored my world. But now, I am unmoored. Nothing is anchoring me at all.

CHAPTER 6

In the morning, my women's group arrives with bagels and cream cheese, vegetables and dips, grape leaves, deli meats, fruit, fancy cheese and crackers, dark chocolate, and four flavors of ice cream. Ricky, Susan, and Diane bustle around my kitchen, setting out plates and glasses.

I sit and watch.

Evidently, I am now in a house of mourning.

"I can't eat," I say in apology as I stare at the spread of food. I look up at them. "I can't read, either." I laugh, slightly hysterical. "I've gotten through all the worst times in my life with books, and now I can't read."

I can tell how strangely I am acting by the concern on their faces.

"I don't want to lose my joy," I continue. "With Perry, I found joy in being alive, in being who I am. I don't want to lose that. I don't want to be bitter and shut down." As I say it out loud, I realize how true this is. More than losing Perry, I don't want to lose this joyful, funny, not-taking-myself-too-seriously version of me, the willing-to-have-adventures kind of person.

Right away, they name all the comedies they can think of about lost love and foolish men leaving amazing women. They want me to know I am not alone.

I think about my nights ahead: movies, wine, cigarettes. "I don't want to spend my last years drunk and demented, coughing up a lung," I hear myself say. And because these women have known me forever, they know what I mean.

***

When I was seventeen and just back from a summer exchange program in India, my extended family celebrated a cousin's wedding at the Veteran's Hall in Queens, New York. During the reception, my mother slapped my father across the face on the dance floor. My sister-in-law took me into the bathroom.

"I should tell you. While you were away, we all found out that your father was having an affair."

I stared at her.

"For many years," she added.

My father left my mother a year later, during my first semester of college.

After that, my mother drank vodka after dinner. On the rocks. On my next visit home, we sat together at the kitchen table while my mother lit one cigarette after another and sipped her drink.

"Your brothers never call," she complained.

"Why don't you call them?" I countered.

She flicked away the question and raked her fingers through her short dark hair that had only sprinkles of gray. Her lips pursed around her cigarette, emphasizing her sculpted cheekbones. She'd often said with pride that people told her she was the image of Katherine Hepburn.

"Other men have affairs and stay married," she said. "Why not him?" She lit the wrong end of her cigarette. The filter burst into acrid flames. "I handled everything," she continued bitterly, stubbing out the cigarette. "Where was your father when your brother John broke his leg?"

"Mom, let's go to bed."

"You go to bed if you want. I'm not tired." She poured more vodka. "Sometimes I wish you children were never born."

I couldn't believe she spoke those words. Disgusted and not at all sympathetic, I stayed tethered to the table, unable to leave, worried she'd burn the house down.

"I think you should find a job," I suggested to her over coffee the next morning. This was 1972. The women's movement was in full swing. I was young, judgmental, and dismissive. Did she actually need a man to feel whole? Why couldn't she just pick up her life and get on with it? In my college apartment, a poster on the wall read, *A woman without a man is like a fish without a bicycle.* I wanted my mother to claim her power.

I wasn't totally insensitive, though. I invited her and a friend to join me on a trip to Puerto Rico over winter break. I found her a therapist. She attended one session and never went back. "The therapist said it was normal to be angry. But I'm not angry," she told me.

I didn't understand the extent of her pain. I was eighteen years old. My sympathy was limited not only by my age but also by our relationship. We'd never been close, her anger a gale wind fueled by resentments I could only guess at, and so I tried to sidestep and avoid.

Looking back, I cringe at my arrogance.

Today, I wish I could say, "Mom, how awful to spend a lifetime with someone, raise children, greet grandchildren, and then have that person not want you anymore." I wish I could acknowledge the pain she must have felt.

I'd often disparaged my mother as superficial (in my twenties, I believed this to be a grave and consequential flaw). I described her as a woman who wanted her life to appear like a framed photograph over the mantel, everyone in the frame perfect and happy. All the real-life struggles and conflicts that happened outside the frame or behind the frame were not relevant.

Perhaps I'd had been living my own version of the framed picture with Perry: older couple, finally wise in the ways of love, reveling in each other's presence, sitting by the fire reading their books, peering up occasionally to meet each other's eyes and smile. Possibly I was only focused on the *image* of us, swept up in the story. I wanted the happy portrait.

Or maybe I was too smug. I told my kids as they experienced their heartbreaks that one thing I'd learned about relationships is how fruitless it is to wish the one we love to be different, to change just one or two characteristics that annoy or irritate us, or to fix just one teeny flaw in their personality. By the time Perry and I married, I thought both he and I had reached this acceptance. I believed we were trying to truly know each other, not change each other. We rarely fought. When we did have conflicts, I believe we handled them well.

But perhaps, like my mother, I relied too much on the picture of what I wanted to see. Dismissing what went on outside the frame as irrelevant, I decided that if it appeared fine, it must be fine.

Perry smiled with contentment when I looked at him. Apparently, when he was off camera, outside the frame, he was a different person entirely, consumed with unspoken desires and wishes.

CHAPTER 7

A week after Perry leaves, I carry my morning coffee up to my desk in the loft, determined to get a start on my monthly client and billing reports. I hold my mug with both hands to warm them. It is glazed in varying shades of blue that remind me of the ocean. I stare out the window, mesmerized by the diverse tones of green as the oaks, maples, beech, and birch leaf out. All the different hues. I don't usually notice such things. Some new chunk of my brain has taken charge and is saying: *Stop. Pay attention. The world is bigger than your aching head and rattled heart.*

My phone rings, and I let it go to voicemail. It's a friend from my writers' group. She leaves a message to remind me that waking up and getting dressed each day is enough of an accomplishment. Nothing more is required during this time. I glance down at my sweatpants and T-shirt. Even at this, I have failed. For days, I've been sleeping and walking through the hours in the same clothes.

Time has slowed way down and each day lasts forever, but it's only been one week since Perry left. I remind myself that I have suffered a shock, and I give myself the same advice as my therapist-self would give to a client. *Go easy on yourself. Take care of yourself. Don't expect to barrel through tasks and chores efficiently.* I am used to prodding myself forward, but now I'm not sure what forward is.

All I can envision for my future are more wrinkles and age spots, with my mind disintegrating, while alone and unaccompanied. All the advertisements, all the messaging, and the entire American culture promote this negative vision I hold. *Look younger: this cream will erase wrinkles. Lose that saggy belly in weeks with our special program. Look younger, or you will end up sad, diminished, and regretful.*

Last night—well, actually at 3:47 this morning—I gave up on trying to sleep and rewatched *The First Wives Club*, pleased I could push buttons and stream movies for distraction in the middle of the night. This film felt like a visit with old friends. When I first saw it, I was in my early forties. I felt so sorry for these characters, which are throwbacks to an earlier era when husbands leaving meant a destroyed sense of self-worth for the wives.

Huddled on the left side, my side, of the king-size bed, surrounded by pillows so I couldn't see the great empty expanse of the rest of it, I watched Goldie Hawn, Bette Midler, Diane Keaton, and Stockard Channing cope with their husbands leaving them for younger women. Their despair and rage, laced with humor, eventually give way to recapturing their sense of self. Together, they forge ahead, creating new lives and purpose. They start a revenge club, which develops into a larger resolve and creates a crisis center for women.

Now, I envy these fictional characters. Their anger is clear, piercing, and energizing. I want to feel the fierce rage that will propel me forward. But I don't. My anger is blunted by love, confusion, and disbelief.

Of course, a man who could walk out on his wife after fourteen years, with no thoughts of what that means to their respective futures financially, emotionally, or logistically, deserves my anger. A man who has lived in partnership without even hinting at this potential, who has hidden himself so completely, deserves my rage.

But that is not Perry. That is not the man I love. So I don't feel anger. It would be like being angry at a kitten who climbed up the shelves in the bathroom, knocking down the moisturizer bottle, toothpaste, and perfume on his way up, and got stuck on top of the medicine cabinet and mewed because he couldn't climb down. He created a huge mess that needed cleaning up, but that wasn't the kitty's intent. He was only exploring, curious, wondering what was up there.

My eyes ache. All I want to do is climb back into my pillow sanctuary and sleep. I sip my coffee and stare at the reports that need writing. Tomorrow, I have to drive to Maine to see clients. And anyway, Perry can't be having the stereotypical midlife crisis. Sixty is *not* middle-aged. He insists he has *not* left me for a younger woman. He's left to *find* another woman, albeit one young enough to have his babies.

Now, I *do* have to finish paperwork. In the agency I work for, my earnings are a combination of salary and consulting fees. This means that if I don't go to work and run the offender groups in Maine, I will not get paid. No sick days, no personal days, no vacation days. I can't afford to take time off.

I close my computer, feeling like I have vertigo from being in the loft so high above the ground and consumed with self-pity. I carry my computer and coffee downstairs. Seated on the couch, I open the computer to the report I need to write and try again. I close the computer and go into the kitchen to pour more coffee, moving as though heavy weights are strapped to my legs. Back at the couch, I open my computer again. My thoughts won't leave me alone.

I know happy-in-love sixty-year-old men don't wake up one morning and decide they want babies. When did Perry start thinking about this? A few months ago, as we kissed by the Trevi Fountain in Rome? Or maybe a few years earlier, when my grandchildren came? It's possible he's been having an affair with a woman still young enough to birth babies, and *she* wants a baby.

I force my mind back to the reports. I write two lines and get up and wipe the kitchen counters. Stare into the open refrigerator, then close it before choosing anything to eat. I do this for hours, writing a few sentences between watering the plants, straightening pillows, loading the dishwasher. A total waste of a day. The reports are not written, and the house has not been cleaned. I've gained no clarity or understanding.

As the day winds down, and I no longer have the energy to even pretend I'm working, I call Perry. He does not pick up. He's been dodging my calls. I pour a glass of wine. I hit redial repeatedly. I pour more wine. By the time he answers, I am crying. It is the first time I have wept, the alcohol loosening me.

"Are you having an affair?"

"No."

"*Did* you have an affair?" I am desperate. I need some familiar trope to hold onto. People fall in love with other people. This happens.

"No. No affairs." He sighs as if we've gone over this ground way too many times already. But we haven't. When I left my first husband, it was not because of new love. It was because of wretched unhappiness.

I can't catch my breath. Does this mean Perry has been wretchedly unhappy while I thought we were so joyful? That would be worse than his having an affair. My body would float away, and my whole sense of reality would be gone. "Please tell me what's happening." I hate the sound of my begging.

"If I told you, you'd never talk to me again," he says, and hangs up. It's only been a week, and this hanging up when I ask questions has become infuriatingly common. I call back, frantic, but he doesn't answer. What did he mean, *If I told you, you'd never talk to me again?*

I become unhinged. I imagine he has done something

unspeakable. I work with men who have committed all kinds of crimes. Some of my clients were caught with child pornography on their computers. I know Perry watches porn occasionally, and I have no issue with that. These clients spoke of easily slipping into dark, illegal territory online as if they had skidded on ice. It could be something like that—a work audit where he got caught with compromising downloads on his computer. He would be so ashamed; he would never tell me. In the field, we don't call it *child porn* anymore. We call it *child sexual exploitation*.

Clients have described arriving home one evening to find that all of their computers and Internet-equipped devices had been seized for investigation. They often then waited years before they were arrested and charged with anything, due to the slow wheels of the justice system. During this time, some never spoke a word about it to anyone.

I picture Perry's computer at school being seized. Is he under investigation for being sexually inappropriate with a student? What else could he possibly have done that would cause me to never talk to him again?

Maybe he has a terminal disease or at least a severely debilitating illness. Maybe he's being noble and trying to save me from going through that with him.

I call a friend to run this theory by her. I am desperate to believe in something that means he didn't leave because of me—because of not loving or wanting *me*.

"No, he's just gone nuts," my friend says matter-of-factly. "He's afraid of getting old. Turning sixty made him frantic. It happens to a lot of men."

I contemplate this theory. Why does fear of aging drive men to want younger women? Obviously, people are afraid of aging because they don't want to die. If young women find an old man attractive, does that mean he's not old? If a young man found me sexually attractive, would that mean I wouldn't die?

If his issue is fear of dying, did I play a part in it? When Perry turned sixty, we celebrated with that much-longed-for trip to Italy, exploring Rome and Tuscany. But before we left, I focused on updating our living wills and choosing a medical power of attorney. I investigated green burials. I wanted to make sure all this paperwork of aging was done so that we could continue with the pleasure of living. Maybe it was too much. Maybe it scared Perry into realizing he will eventually die.

I climb into bed, spent from my wheels ceaselessly turning. Miraculously, I fall asleep but wake at 2 a.m. This time, I watch *Something's Gotta Give*. Diane Keaton plays a fifty-something divorcée who's not interested in love and yet ends up falling in love with an older man (played by Jack Nicholson) who has a reputation for never dating anyone over thirty. After their fling, he summarily dumps her. I laugh as she sobs and types her way through the breakup, tossing tissues to the floor while writing what will be a highly acclaimed play. I feel comforted by her sobs. I am not alone in my abject misery. I am not pathetic! I'm inspired by how she writes through her sobbing. Yet I also find myself judging her character for carrying on after such a short time together. Perry and I had fourteen years! Later in the movie, a younger man falls for her (she is Diane Keaton, after all), but she ends up with Jack Nicholson, who eventually returns to declare his love.

A large part of me believes Perry will walk back in that door and say how much he misses me, wants me, wants our life together. He will say how he went a little nutty and is so sorry. Various friends have even said this. "Oh, he'll be back by the end of summer."

I fall back asleep and wake up to the same reality. Nothing has changed.

***

Leaving the house for work is such a daunting prospect, I'm tempted to cancel. I can't get warm, can't eat, can't sleep. These are all symptoms of shock. I know they will pass. I force myself into the shower.

An email arrives from Perry.

He writes that he's often crying. He explains that he's doing what he thinks will make him happy in the long run. He tells me that we are both going to be happy and fine. He adds: *You have nurtured such a wonderful group of friends and family.*

Fuck you.

My reaction to his condescension is immediate.

Wrapped only in my towel, I reply.

> *Perry,*
> *I know you are doing what you think will make you happy. And I hope that it all works out for you. I love my children, grandchildren, and friends, but they are NOT my life. My life was with you. My future was with you. I trusted you. Please stop trying to make yourself feel better by telling me that I have friends and family. If I had wanted my life to revolve around friends and family, I would never have moved to New Hampshire to be with you.*

CHAPTER 8

On weekends during our first summer together, when Perry and I weren't busy not finishing movies, we traded stories, revealing layers of our past lives as we walked on beaches up and down the Seacoast. I learned that "the Seacoast" is shorthand for the area of the Northeast where three states meet: the North Shore of Massachusetts, the greater Portsmouth area in New Hampshire, and southern Maine. I'd lived in the Boston area my entire adult life and somehow missed this part of the world.

Our first movie date was a somber, subtitled German art film, *Winter Sleepers*. We held hands in the dark. I was distracted by my arousal as his thumb swept back and forth over my palm.

"Did you like it?" he asked as we left the theater.

"To be honest, I'm more of a lowbrow-movie woman," I replied.

He laughed. We went out for dinner and kissed in the rain on the median strip of Massachusetts Avenue in Cambridge.

It was odd meeting someone new later in life. Whole lives had already been lived. It was like beginning a novel smack in the middle.

In his studio apartment in New Hampshire, books were everywhere. Two walls were brick, and the ceilings were high with exposed beams and pipes. Books lined the rafters, filled the bookshelves, and lay in piles on the floor. History books, biographies, novels, and an old musty edition of *Moby Dick*. How could I not like this man?

He also had a collection of VHS movies. As I read the titles of romantic comedies like *The Paper* (1994) with Michael Keaton and Marisa Tomei, I smiled. A kindred lowbrow spirit.

Next to a floor-to-ceiling window was a desk. In the middle of the room, serving as a divider between the kitchen and living room, sat a futon couch that opened to a double bed.

I wonder now if I mistook what happened on that bed for real love. Post-divorce dating can often evoke our inner adolescent, bringing us back to a teenage state. We get drawn to that time of hormones and lustful obsession. After the death of a marriage, a new relationship can be dizzying and intoxicating, flooding the brain with dopamine. Perhaps I was so dazed by the sexual abandon I felt that it shaded everything about how I perceived Perry. For a woman who'd come of age in the 1960s, during the era of free love, I was woefully inexperienced.

***

My first husband and I met when I was fifteen, a sophomore in high school in a suburb outside New York City. Dan was a senior. I think I loved the idea of Dan more than the actual Dan. This may have been true for him as well. Maybe this is true for all first loves.

Dan was long-haired, scruffy, and radical. This was the fall of 1968, a time of Vietnam War protests, the civil rights movement, the assassinations of Martin Luther King, Jr. and Robert Kennedy, hippies, and head-bashing at the Chicago Democratic Convention. Dan was impertinent, rebellious, and aggressively unconventional. He had poor manners with adults, was incapable of small talk, thumbed his nose at authority, dropped acid, and smoked dope. He was brilliant (or so he said) and a certified member of Mensa.

He was my bad boy. Maybe when girls stop having to be good girls, we will stop being attracted to bad boys.

Dan wanted to change the world and make it a better place.

My friends and I all shared the same goal, but I was captivated by Dan's commitment to actually doing so. Eventually though, much of his passion to fix the world would be directed at changing me. Like many men from that era, Dan was angry. He believed he knew what was best for everyone if only people would shut up and listen.

We had our first son when I was twenty-one and Dan was twenty-three. I intended to never marry. I truly believed that if I didn't, I would not slide into all the preordained roles that marriage implied. We could live together and be monogamous. When I got pregnant, we held firm to this conviction.

We called our parents. "I'm having a baby but not getting married," I said to my mother. "You can spread the news."

She just said okay. Even though I was pregnant, I think she was glad I wasn't marrying. She wasn't fond of Dan.

When Dan told his father, he acted as if he was having a heart attack. His mother insisted I get on the phone. "You can't have a baby out of wedlock," she shrieked.

Dan worried about his parents. "If it's no big deal that we don't get married, why is it a big deal if we do?" he reasoned.

"Fine."

I called my mother back. "Can you throw me a wedding? How about the weekend of May eighteenth? Classes will be done."

Talk about presumptuous. But my mother took it in stride and spoke to our neighbor who liked to have parties in her house, and with another neighbor organized the platters of cold cuts. My mother decorated with azaleas and rhododendrons from the May gardens.

Looking back now, I see a pattern. If I pretended something was no biggie, if I tossed it into a corner of my life, then I could avoid feeling worried or anxious. It allowed me to make huge life-changing decisions without acknowledging fear or doubt, but also without much thought or consideration of consequences. For years, I never referred to Dan as *my husband*. I refused to wear a ring. I was not *given away* at my wedding. As if all these tiny rebellions could prevail against the forces of the institution. As if the forces of the institution were what made us so unsuited for each other.

Dan was not an easy man to live with. He managed his emotions by trying to control his environment. As a therapist, I now know this is not unusual, but at the time, I had no clue. All I knew was that he was angry, critical, demeaning, dismissive, competitive, and domineering. We fought often and loudly: over the kids, feminism, money, sex, housework. Fighting was something Dan had grown up with. I had not. It jangled my nerves. It had me sliding down closed bathroom doors weeping, confiding in friends, and hoping desperately that couples therapy could fix us.

When Dan and I separated, our oldest son Orion had just gone off to college. Zac was fifteen, and Josh was twelve. I was thirty-nine and a newly minted therapist.

My brother John had died a few years earlier, leaving a wife and three kids. When their children entered college, his widow, Louise, moved back to the West Coast where she was from. I lived on the East Coast where her kids were attending school, so they stayed with me, and I became a home base for my two nephews and my niece.

For years, I had six kids, initially ranging in age from twelve to twenty-two, living with me. They came and went on adventures, took gap semesters, moved out, moved back in. I was a youngish matriarch of a large clan. I shepherded this group of a half-dozen individuals into adulthood.

At the time, I just went with it. It felt gratifying. I loved the kids. I loved being single. My household was full and boisterous. In the same way that I was good at helping my clients, I believed I was good at raising children, listening and being there for them.

Only later would I think about how much I did during those years, how hectic and chaotic it all was. A circus.

During that time, I dipped my toe into dating every once in a while, when friends set me up—but since Dan and I met so young, I had never actually dated before. I wasn't adept at it. I didn't have the rhythm right. I was either too standoffish or too intense. I remember one man, whom I'd seen twice, calling me on Thanksgiving to invite me out. He knew my sons were with their father, and I was alone. It was considerate, but I was annoyed. It felt intrusive. I was not ready to have someone in my life in that way. Instead, I went out with two single friends to a silly movie, and afterward, over pizza, we joked about our pretend boyfriends. They were much easier to cope with. But Ricky would remind me: "You know, potential lovers don't walk the streets of suburbia knocking on doors. You have to get out there."

So, when all my twenty-somethings had moved into their own apartments, and Josh had left for college, I decided, at forty-six, that I was too young to close up shop. I told the kids: "No one, no way, by accident or on purpose, gets pregnant until Josh graduates." I needed kid-free time.

Ricky helped me write the personal ad I placed in the *Boston Globe*. This was before smartphones and dating apps, and for a year, I had a crash course in dating. I learned to flirt and joke during initial coffee dates without acting as if I was conducting an interview for a job with security-level clearance. With a few men, I even went out a second time, but no one tempted me enough for a third.

I was now a program director at a domestic violence prevention agency. Eight of us worked in a three-room office, and the director and assistant director were close friends of mine. My recent year of seriously venturing into the dating world became fodder for office storytelling.

I didn't want to marry again, as I repeated often. But I wouldn't mind a romance, a fling. Still, all these coffee dates were debilitating. Picking outfits, shaving legs, putting on makeup, attempting to enthrall. And that was after weeding out the truly bizarre and creepy over the phone.

"What do you mean you don't want to meet because there's a restraining order against me? I didn't do anything," more than one indignant man said to me.

And so, it was not with great enthusiasm that I scheduled a meet-up after work with a guy named Perry. I was tired, having pulled an all-nighter driving home from Josh's college debut as director of theater production and then working all day. I did not want to do this date. I thought about standing him up, but Ricky told me that was unacceptable. I had no way to cancel. I knew he had driven down from New Hampshire for this coffee date. I resolved I would keep it short.

At 5 p.m., my colleagues collectively told me I looked fine, had nothing stuck in my teeth, and pushed me out the door.

We were meeting at Wordsworth, a bookstore in Harvard Square. He told me he'd be wearing a green jacket. I stood perusing the new releases, watching people walk in. An elderly gentleman in a green jacket hobbled down the stairs, and I quickly turned away as if utterly engrossed in the book I held. I was aghast. The man had to be eighty.

But he gave a shout and waved to a white-haired woman. I went back to scanning the stacks with guilty relief.

I glanced up again when I heard footsteps. A man in an army-green windbreaker walked down the stairs, glancing over at the new releases. He had a full head of wavy light-brown hair. He saw me and tilted his head in a question.

"Ginny?"

I nodded. "Perry?"

He had blue eyes and was clean-shaven, showing dimples when he smiled. I could smell Old Spice.

He suggested we go to Café of India down the street. I told him, rather primly, I'm sure, that I only did coffee dates when meeting someone for the first time. He nodded as if in agreement and mentioned that appetizers and tea were almost the same as a coffee.

Knowing Perry as I do now, he'd probably driven down early and scouted out the restaurant and bookstore and planned it all out.

I enjoyed the samosas. Perry laughed easily and had deep lines around his eyes. I liked his smile, and he made me laugh. He talked about his experience as a teacher working with middle school students. He told me he'd kept in touch over the years with many of his students and their families. I found this continuity appealing.

"I work with men who have been convicted of battering," I said. "And I also work with the women they've hurt." I had learned that whenever I rattled out these sentences, long conversations could follow about how any woman could accuse any man of anything these days. Alternatively, my job description could end the conversation altogether.

Perry was simply curious, his questions thoughtful and intelligent. *How does the program work? What exactly do you do?*

I liked this man.

"Why are you dating in Boston?" I asked him. "They don't have women in New Hampshire?"

He mumbled something about someday wanting to live in Massachusetts.

"Well," I said, "just so you know upfront, I never intend to marry again, and I will never leave Boston."

He nodded as if this made sense to say on a coffee date. I didn't know it then, but that nod, that serene expression of concerned understanding, was something he employed when facing someone who expressed strong emotion for no clear reason he could identify. Later, I would notice this at his school with the teacher with whom he shared a classroom. She tended to exclaim and sigh and rush around in a dither, emotions on high. I would watch Perry go still, appearing to listen and sympathize. Later, at home, he would tell me how this teacher alarmed and panicked him with her intensity. Somehow, I never recognized that if he could hide his true feelings with her so well, he could also do it with me. At the time, it never entered my mind.

Perry and I did all the things people claim to like doing in personal ads. He took me for a walk on Long Sands Beach in York, Maine. Long Sands is a strip of beach bordered by a sidewalk with houses dating back to the turn of the last century. At low tide, the beach is wide, with tidal pools nestled along the rocks. Up on the bluff is the Nubble Lighthouse. As we ate oysters and watched the sunset, I was in my own rom-com.

A few months later, we went to the deCordova Sculpture Park and Museum in Lincoln, Massachusetts, and wandered among the sculptures. Sitting on the bench underneath a sculpture of two giant entwined hearts, Perry told me he thought he was falling in love with me.

"Wow," I said. "You are a brave man."

I was impressed by his courage to be so honest and vulnerable. Part of me still thinks it was brave, but I probably shouldn't have been so impressed. Maybe he regularly used those lines to move things along.

CHAPTER 9

Day eight. Perry calls me at work as I'm finishing up lunch. "We need to be divorced by September."

"Divorce ordinarily takes longer than three months," I reply coolly. I brush crumbs off my desk.

"Well, if I'm going to start a family, I need to get on it. I'm not getting any younger."

I squelch the urge to laugh, and it comes out as a snort. "It takes more than a summer to find someone who wants to marry and have babies," I say. Increasingly, I am convinced he already has someone. I want him to admit it. There's nothing else it could be. No sane person thinks he'll only need a summer to meet someone and start a family. My worries about dementia return.

We hang up, and I investigate New Hampshire divorce law and find out that either party can file, and there is no waiting period. It occurs to me that I should hire a lawyer. And change the locks. Only a week ago, having such thoughts would have been unfathomable. Rapid change isn't healthy, and it creates a sensation of being transported to a misshapen world.

Somehow, I make it through the workday—but when I get to my car that evening, I begin to cry. I sob the entire way home. Declaring a divorce date for September makes his leaving real and our ending real. The pain is piercing.

That night, I take my wine out to the deck. Over the years, I've planted vegetables for the deer and flowers for the grubs, but I eventually created gardens that surround the house.

Perry sends another email.

*I know I have made you feel crazy and at a loss to
understand your life and what used to be our life
together, to know what was and is real. I loved our
life, and even up to the very end, I allowed myself to
enjoy the warmth of how you and I have been. I met
a woman at the airport during my trip to Vietnam. I
felt an attraction; it was romantic. We kissed.*

Some kiss.

I call him. "You're leaving me for a woman you met in an
airport?"

He talks about being on a layover in Manila and meeting
a young Vietnamese graduate student from the U.S. returning
to Vietnam for a visit. He says they had an instant connection.
She invited him to meet her mother. He tells me it was all very
romantic.

"You slept with her?"

"No." His tone is outraged. "She has a boyfriend."

And you have a wife, I think. But I don't say it.

I don't want him to stay because of these conventions: boyfriend, wife. I want him to stay because he can't imagine coming
home to anyone else.

"What about the guidance counselor you mentioned?" I ask.
"The one you felt attracted to, the one you wanted to pursue. How
does she fit into all this?"

"She hasn't returned texts or phone calls since I told her I left
you. I guess there wasn't as much of a connection as I thought. I
have to go," he mumbles. "The traffic is heavy."

I pace after we hang up. My frustration is so high that I want
to smash flowerpots. I want to rip plants out of the earth. Instead,

I go inside and sink into the couch. Perry doles out crumbs of the story and then invariably hangs up when his story fragments contradict one another. He doesn't seem to recognize that after fourteen years, I deserve, at the very least, a complete and accurate narrative from him. Something that goes from beginning to end.

For some reason, I am more disturbed about him calling the guidance counselor to talk about leaving me than his kiss in an airport. The kiss could be impulsive. The call was deliberate and tells me he is moving ahead with his plan.

I'm not naive. I've read innumerable novels about infidelity. I've seen it countless times with my clients. Older men sleep with younger women. This isn't a new story, but it's a painful one. I don't want it to be mine.

I send out a few more emails, letting people know Perry left. There should be a template for this, like invitations on Evite. Perhaps a little cartoon of Perry waving goodbye with a caption: *My sixty-year-old husband has left me for a woman he met at an airport! Please see my wine wish list.*

The next day, I try to focus on logistical matters. I leave Perry a voicemail and outline my questions regarding pension and life insurance. I feel vaguely proud of myself for being on top of the situation.

When Perry calls me back, he informs me that as soon as the divorce is done, I will be removed from his health insurance.

I am so fucked.

"Why do we need to divorce so fast?" I ask, sincerely bewildered. "I'm not even sure I can get on my company's insurance plan. There are conditions and open enrollment issues."

"Well, I could give you some additional time. Otherwise, there's always Obamacare. But I do want to start a family. I will need to be divorced."

"You can't wait until we figure this out?" I don't want him to do anything rash about filing for divorce. "Is this family already started? Is that why you need the divorce so quickly?"

When he abruptly hangs up, I am infuriated and give voice to it. My sound is enormous, bouncing off the walls and out the open windows and down the hill. It shakes the treetops and sends the starlings into mass flight. I don't understand his constant ducking and weaving.

I begin to fantasize about revenge. I'll send him subscriptions to *Healthy Aging* and AARP. I'll include a package of Depends.

But my anger soon fizzles. I once again drink too much wine. I talk to my niece and ask her to make me a CD of somebody-done-me-wrong love songs. Like a teenager, I want a breakup mix.

Despondently, I check my email. The artist who is designing my book cover has sent an email with the final mock-up. I don't care enough to even open it

CHAPTER 10

One morning, the first summer Perry and I were dating, we hit tennis balls at the local high school. I could tell he was surprised at my wicked forehand since I'd told him I hadn't played in decades. In my early teens, my father would take me out on the high school courts and run me from one side to the other. My role was to send the ball directly back to him. I learned to precisely place the ball. I stopped playing tennis at seventeen when I found out about his affair.

In junior high school, I asked my mother how to make boys like me—what was the secret that all the other girls seemed to know? She suggested I should lose at tennis. Boys, she told me, like to win.

I wonder if I appeared too strong with Perry, if I seemed too competent. Perhaps he felt that I didn't "need" him enough and that made him feel inadequate.

But even asking these questions discomfits me. I don't want to be a woman who asks such questions or who hides her strength.

Perry and I both came of age when the roles of women and men were dramatically shifting and changing.

Pronouncements from decades ago about how a woman was supposed to act and what a man was required to be are laughable and ludicrous today. In the late sixties, there were vehement debates in national magazines and on television about whether men and women were actually equal. The argument often went that if men and women *were* equal in brain power and creativity, why were there no major literary works by women, or musical compositions, or paintings in art museums? Why did women have no major achievements in science and math?

At gatherings for dinner with friends and family, people questioned whether anyone would realistically trust a female police officer or a female firefighter.

In junior high, we were tracked into either advanced English and social studies or advanced math and science. My mother suggested the humanities. "Women aren't clever at math and science," she said.

Even in 1974, when I married Dan, women having the right to their own credit card was controversial.

And then this all began to change. Women questioned long-held assumptions, discovered long-buried history, and demanded transformation. For women living through this era, it was exhilarating and mind-blowing. For men, it was mind-twisting. Suddenly, they were being cast in the evil role of perpetrators, supporters of the patriarchy. And all they thought they'd been doing was trying to figure out how to get laid.

I remember a fight with Dan when I came home electrified after one of my first women's studies courses in college.

"What do you mean women have it harder than men?" His long hair tied in a ponytail, he paced the center of our tiny attic apartment, the only place he could stand up straight. "That's the most ridiculous idea I've ever heard."

"Look around." I sat at my desk under the eaves. "All over the world, women are oppressed."

"You're trying to tell me that some poor slob working at a factory job for minimum wage to support his family is oppressing women?" Dan snorted. "Give me a break."

"I'm saying that—"

"Men are oppressed. We are oppressed by the rich and power-ful. And many of the rich and powerful are wealthy *women*."

How could we be arguing about this? It seemed so obvious to me. Arguing with Dan made my head cloudy.

"Women weren't even considered human," I said. "The coun-cil of cardinals voted that women were human by one goddamn vote!"

"That was in the fucking Middle Ages. You're bizarre."

"In 1919, women couldn't vote in this country."

"That was 1919!"

It was a lurchy time. Dan and I struggled through that period when even being asked for a cup of coffee was fraught with over-tones. *Get it yourself; I'm not your servant.*

Perry was of the same generation. But we were a lot older when we met. I had lived alone for many years, raising kids. He had lived alone for many years as well. We were both competent and knew how to take care of ourselves. Doing things for each other was never fraught. He loved to food shop and cook. I was happy to take care of the laundry. He took out the garbage. I vacuumed and straightened the house. He drove when we were together; I did enough driving on my own for work.

I managed the bills. He called the guys to clean out the septic tank. Both of us shoveled the drive.

When Perry and I were still together, I read an article suggest-ing that to increase intimacy, a woman should make her man feel like a hero. I was incensed that in the twenty-first century, this was still being stated. I remember also feeling superior because we didn't have "intimacy" problems.

I loved Perry with abandon. I loved his body. It's not like he had a perfect body; it's just that something in the chemistry of my body connected with his, and I loved every inch of him.

I loved that he was a teacher of English with immigrant middle and high school kids. I loved his politics. I loved his reading lists. I loved that he loved to go to libraries and wander the stacks. I loved spending time with him.

But the truth is, I didn't need Perry to take care of me in any of the traditional male roles. Provider. Money manager. Hunter. Protector. Explainer.

I know he had moments of self-doubt, of feeling less than. When we met, he was in his late forties, a teacher who needed to work summers to make ends meet. He dreamed of writing and creating art, but never quite started. He had no assets, earned little, and had no interest in moving up the public school ladder to principal or superintendent. By many standards of success for males of his generation, he hadn't made it.

By my standards, he was pure gold. Kids came to America from all over the world, speaking no English, landing in middle school, and he, with his calm grace, created a space for them to learn, share their worries, and blossom. They were forever grateful. They returned frequently to visit with their spouses and children and brought stories of their successes.

As we established our life together, I was all in. We would grow old and see each other through to the end. I stepped around his brown bags full of papers. I opened the mail and dealt with the business end of living. He arranged outings and adventures.

For the first time in my life, I relaxed into feeling loved and cared for. I am a good caretaker, whether by temperament, training, or conditioning. But I wasn't as familiar with being cared for. I blissfully sank into the pillow of that comfort.

But not all at once. In the beginning, I was skittish and hesitant.

Perry played tennis doubles three or four times a week with the same group he'd been playing with for years. During our first month together, he brought me to a tennis group barbecue. Frank, one of the senior members of the group, took me aside and grilled me about my intentions. It was disconcerting since I had no idea at that point if I had any intentions, but it was also charmingly endearing. I had learned during this year of dating to avoid men over forty-five with no friends, and at least now I could check that off my list.

"I don't want his heart broken again," Frank said.

Perry had been married for a short time right after college, but Frank was referring to Joanne, Perry's partner of over ten years, who'd died of breast cancer a few years before we met.

When Perry told me about Joanne, he described a scene when she was near the end of her life. Because she could no longer go outside, he gathered all the colorful leaves of autumn onto a large sheet and lay it across the bed where she lay.

This was a man who knew how to care.

CHAPTER 11

Love stories begin, as many of our stories do, in childhood. And my childhood, like many childhoods, was one I couldn't wait to be done with. If we go by the idea that our mothers are our first love and we learn what love means from them, I learned that when a person loves you, they will have many needs. Mostly unspoken. I also determined that I'd better figure out those wordless needs because otherwise, there would be eruptions of high emotion for confusing reasons. My mother would resort to yelling or violence when upset, yet all of this was hidden between us.

Fear was my primary emotion around my mother, although our outward appearance was of a well-behaved daughter and her loving mother. I went to my father's side of the bed when I woke with a tummy ache in the middle of the night. If I couldn't physically distance myself from my mother, I hid from her. Deep inside. So deep that I was hidden even from myself. I knew how to act like a good girl. I was stellar at playing the part.

On my father's side, I grew up in a second-generation Italian family twenty-nine miles outside New York City, surrounded by many cousins, aunts, and uncles. Everyone had dark hair, brown eyes, and loud opinions. I had wild almost black curls and often jumped from subject to subject.

In my 1950s neighborhood on Long Island, grandparents with strong accents from all over Europe visited on Sundays. Most of the parents had finished high school, some had not, and college was something planned for the kids.

The houses were small, the maple trees large, and the yards full of flowers, grass, and kids. These families had all recently moved from Brooklyn and Queens to farther out on Long Island. The adults had survived the Depression and World War II and were content to sit outside sipping cocktails while the kids played hide-and-seek.

My father worked as a salesman in the garment industry on Seventh Avenue in New York City. He traveled long hours to get to work. Years later, I understood it was a source of pride to live in the suburbs. But the cost was great. Every morning, Long Island would float lighter on the Atlantic as the Long Island Rail Road carried all the dark-suited men into the city. My father returned daily on the 6:03 train, and all the energy in the house turned toward him like plants to the sun.

When my family left Brooklyn to land in white suburbia, which Betty Friedan called housewife territory, my mother did her best to fit in. She became a Boy Scout leader and joined the PTA. The sewing basket on the dining room table overflowed with skirts, pants, socks—colorful clothes needing buttons and seam repairs. My mother would reach for the basket when she needed a pin and sigh. "I really should get to this soon." Domestic chores seemed to startle her. She'd look around as if to say, *Me? I'm supposed to do this?*

Every morning before school, my mother brushed my hair. At each stroke, I winced; the skin on my forehead pulled backward while my head followed.

My mother would push my head forward with the heel of her hand. "Keep still. Such gorgeous hair. You can thank me for this hair. Why can't you hold your head still? Are your neck muscles weak? Once you have children, everything goes. That's what your grandmother told me after my father died. She said, first, your waist, your teeth, your hair, and then, of course, your husband who got you into this in the first place."

The bristles pierced my scalp.

"Of course, all young girls think they're different." The hand came, pushing my head forward. "They think, not me. For me, I'll choose a man who'll stay. Or they think, not me, I'll have the charm to make him stay."

At ten, I asked for a pixie haircut.

My brothers were nine and twelve years older than I was. My mother told me that I was an accident, a failure of birth control. Given all the things she didn't talk about, this was a strange piece of information to reveal. I reasoned that this was why I did not bring her pleasure or joy. I also did not have siblings my age. I assumed, as young children do, that there was something wrong with me.

As a therapist, I have treated severely abused children. I hesitate to ever compare myself to them. I only remember one incident. One day, when I was in first grade or so, I was standing on tiptoes in the kitchen, reaching for the milk. In the process, I tipped over a serving bowl containing that night's dinner. My mother swung at me. I ended up across the room, stunned, my back smashed against the cabinets, with my mother crying that I had spilled the stew.

Much, much later, when my mother died, I heard stories I'd never heard before. My brothers, both in their forties at the time, compared abuse memories. Remember how mom threw us down the stairs? Remember how Mom hit us with the chair? Remember how we'd wait outside on the stoop, hoping Dad would show up soon?

I was shocked. They had never told me.

But by most measures, my mother was a good mother and a good 1950s housewife. She cooked, cleaned, kept the house stocked with groceries, ensured we had spotless clothes and fresh sheets, and had our homework done. All of this, I know, is no easy feat with three children.

What about my father in all this? He was kind and charismatic. He worked long, hard hours and took obvious joy in his well-behaved children and orderly household.

He was the kind of person who wore a big smile and invited neighbors over for cocktails at the last minute. He loved to tell stories that were highly embellished and loose on facts.

Our neighbors were the kind of people who were always outside on the weekends, fixing, painting, weeding, lawn mowing, and raking leaves. No one hired help.

My father's way of connecting was jovial, hail-hearty. How's the wife? Bring her over. Life is good, except for those damned Republicans.

And then he would call to my mother, "Edie, I invited the Gisones, the Mallorys, and the Wolfs over for cocktails. Do we have any cheese or crackers?"

And my mother was the kind of person who seethed and muttered under her breath that he never bothered to find out first if having guests was okay with her as she put together cheese and cracker plates, set dinner on low, and quickly changed into a dress and put on lipstick.

At eight, I was the kind of girl who curled into a chair, reading in the next room and listening to the conversations, marveling that so many people could be having so many different ones at the same time in the same room.

My brothers were the kind of teens who came home after their weekend jobs to exclamations and greetings, then took the stairs two at a time to shower and change for their dates.

Over a dinner of dried-out meat (because the neighbors had stayed for just one more) and iceberg lettuce, I would listen as my father expounded about ridiculous politicians and their pointless policies. After dinner, I would be excused to watch my half hour of television before bed, and my brothers would head out for the evening while my mother cleaned up.

I never saw my father angry. I never heard him raise his voice. Ever. My father came from an immigrant Sicilian-Italian family with many children, a mother who spoke no English, and a father who worked as a longshoreman on the docks of New York City. His father became violent when angry or troubled.

My father decided at a young age that he'd be different. When displeased, there was a scowl. That was it. His brow became one long line, his face pulled down, and the wrinkles showed. He did not yell, but the intensity of his disappointment filled the house. He shook his head, rubbed his forehead, and smoothed back non-existent hair, and everyone went quiet and gave him a wide berth. We tried not to cross him.

Now that I have raised three sons and spent a great deal of time with my six grandchildren, I can say with certainty that children are full of emotions. They scream. They tell you that you are unfair. They lose their lovies and collapse in howls of despair and bereavement. They giggle uncontrollably as they do somersaults off the couch. They fight. They hide under the table, refuse to come out, and you have no idea what happened.

In disparate yet related ways, my parents created an environment where the children did not get angry, yell, or complain. We kids never confided in one another about what occurred with our mother when our father was not around. My brothers never told my father or me about any of what they experienced. Once, in high school, my mother was in a rage because I had forgotten to start the water boiling for peas. She berated me. I cried. When the front door opened, we turned to my father in unison, smiling and asking how his day was. Somehow, we knew that to have an emotional scene in front of him would incur that frown.

***

Perry was also raised to keep silent, never talk back, and never express wants and needs, but for different reasons. He grew up in Laconia, New Hampshire, the eldest of five. Both of his parents worked for Bell Telephone. He told me stories of ice fishing on Lake Winnipesaukee, ice skating on ponds, snow sledding on surrounding farms, and playing ball in the streets. He made it sound as idyllic as any stereotype of small-town New Hampshire life.

He'd planned to attend seminary after college, but decided against it and worked several social service jobs instead. He moved to the New Hampshire Seacoast to work for an environmental protection agency and later became an ESOL teacher.

On an early date, he told me that his mother had had debilitating Parkinson's disease. As she became more and more incapacitated, his father would work his shift to support the family and then return home to care for the children and his wife. By the time Perry was twelve, his mother needed to be spoon-fed at the table.

When I asked how this was for him growing up, he shrugged and told me he played a lot of sports. Perry never talked in detail about what it was like to be a young boy with a very sick mother. But I imagine that with four younger siblings, a father who worked full-time, and a mother increasingly unable to care for herself or her children, it would have been near to impossible for him to express *his* needs and wants. Those skills remained undeveloped.

Perry was, however, extraordinarily proficient at caring gestures: smoothing hair, holding hands, stroking skin. He must have used these gestures repeatedly as a teen to communicate love to his ill mother without having to resort to the awkwardness of words. Teenagers, especially boys of that period, struggle to find language to convey affection and compassion.

During our years together, I learned that Perry tended toward mild renderings of expression. When he was angry, he would say quietly that he was frustrated. To me, *frustration* implies slight irritation, but for Perry, it might mean that he was in a white-hot rage. If he said he was worried, it might mean he was about to jump out of his skin with anxiety. I learned to gently probe for more of what was happening behind the façade.

This was such a contrast to my first husband, who'd been raised to fight forcefully for what he wanted. It also contrasted with my father, who ceaselessly pronounced opinions and told stories with flair. It wasn't until much later, after Perry left, that I realized these men were also hiding. All that arguing and expression of certainties served to make sure some internal parts of themselves were never visible.

CHAPTER 12

As a child, I was not cognizant of the power my father's quiet but intense displeasure had on the household. I simply wanted to please him, to generate that wide smile.

However, I knew I was afraid of my mother. I don't think she intended this, but her rages were unpredictable and fierce. I learned early on never to argue, question, or create "a scene." Expressing emotions was dangerous.

I did what she asked without talking back. Ever.

To be fair, by the time I was old enough to have clear memories, my mother did not ask outrageous things of me: empty the dishwasher, put dirty clothes in the hamper, wipe your feet, boil the water for the pasta, make your bed.

Judy was the childhood friend who first questioned my mother.

"I can't come over after school," I said. "I have to be home at four."

"Why?" asked Judy.

I had no idea. It was just the rule.

Why? The little word that changed my life.

I met Judy in 1966, in junior high.

"My friend Ron likes you and wants you to sit with us at lunch," Judy said one day at the end of the eighth period.

"Oh." I was okay with this. Lunch was a problem for me, as I didn't have a best friend to sit with. I was liked well enough in general, but I was not the kind of girl who giggled with her girl-friends, talking about boys, sex, and makeup. In fact, I knew next to nothing about sex. I wasn't super athletic. I had no idea about the right fashion, the latest hairstyles, or the popular music. I'd never tried makeup. And although I'd gotten my period at ten, I had yet to grow breasts.

In fact, nothing much that I could see stood out about me. I loved to read. I wrote long, involved stories about animals escaping captivity. I was anxious in school. I wanted to do well. I was a good girl, the kind of kid teachers liked.

My closest friend from my neighborhood had recently moved away. She and I had spent hours together searching for snakes and box turtles and making habitats for them out of shoe boxes. We rode bikes, climbed the apple tree in my backyard, and read books sitting high on its limbs. These talents didn't translate well to the social skills needed in junior high.

Judy was tall and slender. She had a long face with a square chin and frizzy hair that she attempted to tame into being straight, but it didn't behave. My own curly hair was a daily torment, which I attempted to scotch tape into submission with Dippity-do gel, carefully plastering my bangs to my forehead and taping them down. This was the era when the stick-thin model Twiggy was the epitome of beauty, along with long, sleek, straight hair.

I'd come from Lenox Elementary, a working- to lower-middle-class bunch of kids. Judy came from Brookside Elementary, which was more of a middle- to upper-middle-class bunch of kids.

I don't remember now the sequence of events that propelled our friendship. That year, Judy asked me to go to her home after school, urged me to study together on weekends, and invited me to sleepovers. I had never before had a sleepover.

Judy's father was a doctor. Judy's mother had gone to college, and Judy's grandmother had gone to college. I had not known any parents, not to mention grandparents, who'd attended college. Her parents wanted to be called George and Sally, instead of Dr. and Mrs.

There was always a group of girls over at Judy's house. We all sat together in her room, which was upstairs and very private. I listened as they talked about boys and breasts and bras and hair.

Judy spoke about masturbation. I did not know what the word meant.

"You've never touched yourself?" she asked me.

I had no idea what she was talking about. I must have appeared blank and embarrassed because she quickly switched her tone from disbelieving judgment to educational, the giver of information. She sent me home, suggesting I try it out. "My father says it's normal," she told me. She also suggested I read *Valley of the Dolls.* Thus began my sex education.

At Judy's house, we could go downstairs and fix ourselves a snack whenever we were hungry. At Judy's house, friends were always invited for dinner. At my house, no one could open cupboards to forage, and no dinner invitations were ever issued.

It was Judy who noticed that at my house, my brothers and father spoke of women as attractive or not attractive.

"That's all they care about," she lamented.

"No, it's not."

But when I paid closer attention, it was true.

Judy yelled at her parents. Judy whined. Judy pleaded and begged to be allowed to do things. She stomped and stormed around. She flung herself up the stairs with more drama than any Hollywood actress I'd ever seen. Yet Judy was not punished for any of this. She was allowed to be a kid.

Judy questioned my mother's authority. "Why do you do everything she says?"

The truth was, I wasn't sure. I hadn't thought about it that way.

It was Judy who opened the world to me beyond my parents and family. That's what friends do—introduce each other to sex, drugs, rock and roll.

Eventually, we did all that. But in that first year in eighth grade, Judy introduced me to feelings. And to my body.

Junior high became a tug-of-war between my mother and Judy. I had no clue about my own feelings or my body, but I was a master at understanding tone of voice, certain inflections, and facial expressions. When the phone rang, and it was Judy, my mother's face would darken.

"Why is she always calling you? Didn't you just see her at school?"

My mother didn't stand a chance.

Judy was the first person to talk to me about feminism. Her older sister had told her about something called "the women's movement."

"I don't think women are unequal to men," I told Judy.

"*You* don't. But the rest of the world does."

***

During college, I often spent summers with Judy in Cambridge, Massachusetts, where she attended school. We'd hang out at the Women's Center on Prospect Street. One summer, we joined a new study group called Our Bodies/Ourselves. The founders were hoping to reclaim medical information specific to women. The authors had published a pamphlet that would grow to become an international best-selling book for years. We inspected our cervixes with speculums and mirrors. We announced our feminism with hairy armpits, hairy legs, and frizzy hair on our heads. We refused to conform to the cultural and commercial norms of what beautiful women were supposed to do or look like. We wore hiking boots with long dresses. We wore T-shirts and cargo shorts and never used makeup. We were proud. We were radical. We were tough.

But sometimes, on rainy afternoons, we would go to the drugstore and buy fake nails. I'd pick out polish colors while Judy watched, making sure no one we knew was there to see us. We'd slink up to the cashier, slide the files, nails, and polish across the counter, and run back to the apartment, clutching our bag of contraband as if we'd pulled off a great heist.

We'd turn on the TV (Judy loved old *Perry Mason* reruns), climb onto the bed, and lay out our supplies. Carefully, we'd glue talons onto our fingers. By the time we had nails on one hand, getting the nails on the other was almost impossible. Later, we'd polish—usually bright red, sometimes bubblegum pink. We'd wave our nails to dry them, hooting and giggling.

***

After college, when Dan and I moved to Boston with our first-born, Judy and I would meet up daily. I held Orion in a front pack while we walked or sat in a coffee shop for hours. Back in my apartment, she cared for the baby while I napped.

It was Judy who suggested I needed to be with other moms. At the time, Dan and I lived in the student ghetto in Allston. I would wake up at 2 a.m. to nurse Orion and watch through the window as the college kids partied across the alley. I was twenty-one, and none of my peers had children or were even close to thinking of them. Most women I knew were forging ahead with the second wave of feminism, applying to medical school or law school or building careers.

Judy found me a mothers' group. The women I met there would become my women's group that continues to meet over forty years later.

Judy fell in love with a woman named Julie, left Boston, and moved to New Hampshire. We couldn't hang out as often, but when we did—and we did as often as we could—it was Judy I went to with worries about my children, marriage, or extended family. And Judy came to me to talk about the community she'd formed, the daughter they were raising, and her diagnosis of breast cancer at forty-five.

Judy would have been the one with whom I explored the meaning of Perry leaving. Judy would have helped reorient me.

She died the year before I met Perry.

CHAPTER 13

It's Saturday, and it's only nine days since Perry left. Another goddamn beautiful day. I wish for raging storms with driving rain to better match my mood. But no, the sun shines, the temperature rises to the seventies, and a warm breeze gently wafts the leafing trees.

I send Perry an email.

> *This is all so astounding. It's bad enough you left*
> *our 14 years over email. But you have expressed*
> *no awareness of the impact of your decision on my*
> *well-being or my future. Your apparent obliviousness*
> *to my feelings, my financial well-being, my having*
> *to create a new future, my ability to function, and*
> *my sense of what trust and love mean at 61 years old*
> *astounds me. Who is this man who refuses to talk*
> *after doing such a thing to someone he purported to*
> *love as recently as last week?*

I immediately get a reply.

> *I do not plan to call to talk when you are as upset as*
> *you seem to be; I am willing to plan a later time to*
> *talk by phone or in person.*

I stare at this email. What a fucker! Really? I can't fathom how he dares to play the victim here.

Anger propels me off the couch and into the gardens, where

I wrench weeds from the soil and, in my fury, likely a few young plants. In the spring, at the beginning of the growing season, it's often impossible to tell the invasive and destructive weeds from the seedlings that need to be nurtured into bloom.

***

During our first summer together, when we were still in the seedling phase of our relationship and didn't yet know if we'd bloom, Perry took me to meet his sister and nieces in Saco, Maine. She served lobster and seemed so pleased that Perry had brought someone to meet her. His nieces giggled. I was charmed.

In Boston, I invited my three sons, my niece, and a nephew to meet him. I was nervous. I'm sure they were as well. My ex-husband, Dan, had remarried, but in seven years, I had never brought a man around. I cooked lasagna and hoped for the best. My crowd of twenty-something kids was loud. They talked over each other and laughed often; they could argue about anything and always did. They were brilliant and exuberant but not yet sure of their place in the world.

"He seemed nice. Didn't say much," was the verdict from the kids.

"There was a lot of testosterone flying around," Perry commented.

Soon, I introduced him to my women's group, Ricky, Susan, and Diane.

Perry and I were vetting our relationship: I think this person is incredible, amazing, glorious. What do you think? Is he merely a weed that should be pulled and tossed? Is my judgment clouded?

Everyone liked him. Everyone was happy that I was happy.

For the next three years, we traveled back and forth between our places, spending weekends at his apartment in Dover, N.H., or at my condo in Boston. It was a luxurious realm of lovemaking, reading, and cooking. Then, during the week, we each went back to our responsibilities.

If I were to direct the movie version of those first years, it would be a montage of images to help the viewer quickly get through the early parts of a romance and into the nitty-gritty. He took me cross-country skiing for the first time in College Woods, kissing and laughing as the snow fell. We used anniversaries (the first time we met, the first time we made love, the first time we traveled together) as excuses for weekend excursions. Foolish with romance, we made love in the elevator of the Museum of Fine Arts. On Sundays, we read the whole *New York Times* and *Boston Globe* cover to cover, entwined on my couch.

In between those images of us, there would be me in my condo in Boston during the week, dancing to sappy love songs—Emmylou Harris and Don Henley—dashing to work, having dinner with the kids, and writing at the coffee shop around the corner on Center Street in Jamaica Plain. I was *happy*.

Like every lover since the dawn of time, I believed Perry and I had invented love. As Chani Nicholas wrote, whenever love strikes, we are new born, split open, vulnerable, and naked. Terrified, exalted, alive, I screamed, *Yes*. Colors were brighter, taste was exquisite, and emotions rampant.

I thought of myself as falling in love, but actually, I was dragged. The other parts of me—the part that had three grown sons, the part that worried about money, grocery shopping, work deadlines, and practicalities—said, *Stop!*

I wasn't sure I was ready for this.

We lived over an hour and a half away from each other. That suited me fine. I could be ensconced in a romantic couple on weekends and independent on weekdays. Unlike younger people hoping to find the person they'd build a life and perhaps have children with, we didn't need this relationship to rush anywhere in particular.

Once, as I drove back to Boston after a trip with the kids and was hurrying to get to a meeting, Perry called to tell me he had driven down to surprise me at my condo. Unease flared. It felt presumptuous. *Don't invade my life.* My self-reliance had been hard-won, and I wasn't yet persuaded I wanted to relinquish it.

I resisted the trappings of coupledom. Even later, after we moved in together, I made sure I had a writing class and my own friends in New Hampshire. Traveling to Boston weekly, I was determined to maintain my relationships with friends and colleagues there. I would not be the kind of person who isolated herself in a couple bubble, who neglected all her previous connections once she found love. I wanted my life to be full, abundant.

But fourteen years later, when Perry left for his trip to Vietnam, I was startled by tinges of apprehension. Even though I was excited to have unfettered time to finish my book, a part of me did not want to be alone with the snow, with the driveway, with myself, in the elongated December darkness.

While he was on that trip, I knew I'd become part of a couple in a way I'd been denying. I had grown comfortable in every way with having Perry in my life.

When I remember this now, it seems so sad and not a little ironic. While his trip had him deciding to shift away from me, I recognized that I finally had fully committed.

CHAPTER 14

After my mother died, my father told me my maternal grand-mother had been an alcoholic. She would start drinking Friday evenings after work, pass out, and then wake up to continue drinking through the weekend until she had to get up and go to work on Monday morning. He also told me that my mother's father had been married before and had two other daughters. The reason my grandmother had been left penniless and homeless when my grandfather died was that the life insurance money went to his first family.

After Perry leaves me, I realize I come from a line of women who'd been left to manage on their own as best they could. As a feminist, I am astounded at how little I know of the women who came before me.

When my first son was born in 1974 and my mother visited me in Boston, I took her to a consciousness-raising meeting at the Cambridge Women's Center. I hoped she would easily become an empowered feminist and be happy so I wouldn't have to worry about her anymore. I also hoped she might open up more.

It was a structured meeting, meaning there was a leader and a topic. The topic happened to be our mothers. When we left, my mother turned to me and said, "At some point, people have to stop blaming their mothers and make their own lives." I assumed she was instructing me to stop blaming her for any of my shortcomings.

In hindsight, I wish I had asked her more about her relationship with *her* mother. I did try, but she'd deflect, change the topic, and give few answers. I wish I had pressed her.

The little I did know was bleak. After my mother's father died when she was nine years old, she and her mother were homeless, sleeping on the couches of various relatives. This was during the Depression. By the age of ten, she was taking care of her alcoholic mother as best she could.

My mother was a beauty. Dark, almost black, wavy hair, high cheekbones, large hazel eyes. Pictures of her in her teens take my breath away.

I know it's not unusual for young, unprotected children like my mother to be sexually abused. As a beautiful young teen, largely on her own, with an alcoholic mother, it is possible she was preyed on. Sexually abused children often carry heavy shame into adulthood and have emotional outbursts they don't understand. They try to pretend everything is normal. It would explain a lot about my mother and her need to have everything in that picture frame at least look fine. It's one of many reasons I regret not talking with her more when I could. But then again, she was so intensely private that I'm not sure she would have answered.

It could be that the clarity I seek about my mother is like the clarity I seek from Perry. I'm frustrated with how truths about people elude and evade us.

And although my father seemed so different from my mother, he, too, was opaque. He liked to expound on the day's news or share his home projects, but neither of my parents spoke openly with their children or with each other about their deferred dreams or disappointments or what they still longed for. This was a function of the time, I know, but when I was a child, it gave me the impression that adults were fully formed, no longer needing to learn anything new or ask questions about how to navigate the world and relationships.

Already, I think my grandkids know me better than I knew my parents. They finish the stories I start. "When I went to first grade, I felt worried," I say to my six-year-old granddaughter, who's nervous about school. I shrug and continue, "Starting new things always makes people a bit nervous. Anyway, the teacher told us: No talking. No talking to friends during class. And I thought that was okay because I didn't *have* any friends. But a few weeks later—"

My granddaughter interrupts my story with a toothless grin and shouts, "You were yelled at for talking to your friends. You made friends!"

I like that my grandchildren interrupt me. I like that we talk. My hope is that knowing a great deal about the desires, failures, and mistakes, as well as the successes and accomplishments, of those who lived before them will allow them to weather—with self-forgiveness—the inevitable ups and downs of their own lives. I want them to know that if we are lucky, our learning goes on forever; and that when faced with sudden shocks or turns in our lives that make us despair with uncertainty, we have the capacity to discover new paths.

CHAPTER 15

A few days later, I wake up to a voicemail from Perry. "Hi, sweetie. Just wanted to let you know today is the field trip to Strawbery Banke. I'll be thinking of you."

Brutal.

I've never known him to be cruel and I cannot understand why he would leave me this message or refer to me as *sweetie*, as though nothing is wrong.

Strawbery Banke, a living history museum on the New Hampshire coast, is one of my favorite places. I've grown to love Portsmouth. At the beginning of my relationship with Perry, I was hesitant to move, but this little city by the sea lured me out of Boston. On days when I'm not working in either Boston or Maine, I walk the brick sidewalks and watch the tugboats. I write in Breaking New Grounds, a coffee shop in Market Square. My writers' group meets a block away on Tuesday nights at the Unitarian church built in the early 1800s. These friends, who feel more like family, have patiently read draft after draft of my novel. Every Friday, we meet at a restaurant for happy hour.

I call Shannon, my hairdresser. My roots are showing. I tell her that Perry left me.

"We will do sexy at sixty," she says as we make an appointment.

I laugh.

I cancel all my work appointments for the day and watch the movie, *It's Complicated*. Alec Baldwin's character has left his first wife, Meryl Streep, for a younger woman. But now, he is missing his old life and wants to have an affair with his first wife. I never watch TV during the day unless I'm truly sick. I decide this qualifies. I laugh hard, especially at the scenes of Alec Baldwin at sixty-ish with a rambunctious and spirited five-year-old.

I am not proud of how gleeful I am thinking of past-middle-age Perry chasing a toddler. Perry, who loves his routines and quiet mornings reading the paper before work. Perry, who likes to suggest various options for the day and then only choosing at the last minute. It's the kind of life people can have only when they are not busy adapting to the needs of young children.

After finishing the movie, I force myself to make lists of things I need to do. That is almost the same as actually doing them.

A few hours later, I receive a string of Perry's weird, brief emails arriving in rapid succession.

> *Our life was happy for a lot of years*

Another:

> *Gin, you gave me so much happiness and confidence*
> *You gave me a renewed belief in myself*

Another:

> *You made me feel so loved, so happy and strong*

Another:

> *With the issue of having children of my own — the*
> *doubts and questions you have raised about this don't*
> *dissuade me from thinking that it is still possible*
> *for me and that there isn't anything wrong with me*
> *wanting to try.*

Oh, yes, there is a reason for dissuading you to try, I think as I wander through the gardens in the fading light. You are too fucking old. You have no money. You're not some rich celebrity who can provide for a family after you die.

Even if he already got someone pregnant, he'd start fatherhood at sixty. If he is honestly only searching for someone, the earliest he'd be a father is sixty-two. If all goes well, he'll be eighty when they graduate high school. Does he fantasize about coaching soccer in his seventies?

When Perry has one bad night's sleep, he's grumpy for the next three days. He's lived his entire adult life catering to his own whims and desires. He knows nothing about having days (and nights) dictated by the decrees of infants and children.

Yep, I decide. He's definitely gone mad.

I go back inside and call him. Of course, he doesn't pick up. I keep punching redial until he does.

"Please tell me what happened to us," I say.

"Oh, Gin." It's almost a moan.

"Why can't you try to get what you want here? With me?"

"You can't give me babies."

No, that I cannot do. "We could adopt!" I say this even when I know it's absurd. Even though I am not remotely interested in raising children from scratch again. There is a reason grandparents love being grandparents. I know adoption at sixty is not in the cards.

"I want a family of my own," he says.

"I wish you triplets!" I say, and hang up.

***

For survival, our brains are hardwired to make sense of patterns. Right now, my brain is stymied, grasping for something that makes sense. By day, I handle business, write lists, go to work, wash dishes, and talk to the people who love me. But by night, I sleep fitfully and wake up to watch rom-coms about men leaving women. The movies follow a familiar pattern: a person is happy in love, then bereft because their lover leaves, then happy in love again as eventually they get back together. Maybe this is why I am drawn to them. It crosses my mind that these are fueling my fantasy that Perry and I will get back together. Might not be the healthiest thing to be doing.

Many evenings, more than I care to admit, I drink too much wine and make weeping calls to Perry, seeking answers.

After Perry told me he wanted a divorce, he must have thought he was past the hard part. He told me he'd been trying to get up the nerve for an unspecified amount of time. He thought he had finally ripped off the Band-Aid. He didn't anticipate that I would have feelings or that he would have to witness those feelings. His level of self-absorption astonishes me.

Everything about his leaving is incomprehensible. We were making plans for the future. Now, he sends me notes about how wonderful our relationship was.

But he is leaving out huge hunks of information: *If I told you the truth, you would never talk to me again.*

This leaves me desperate to fill in the blanks, and I'm an expert at making things up.

I need the actual story, the true one, to know which way to think about this to move forward. If the narrative is "I'm discontented," that could be an opening to possibly saving our marriage.

If the story is "I'm in love with someone else," I will know to weep, wail, rage, and move on.

It's the ambiguity that I can't tolerate. The implausibility of leaving a marriage to make babies at sixty with someone he met in an airport, combined with the crying and the nostalgic messages, is a contradictory, tumultuous mix. I don't know whether to slam the door or keep it open.

***

In my first marriage, I definitively knew when I was ready to leave. The issues and conflicts were clear to both of us. I didn't experience this sort of grief.

Both my marriages lasted many years, but I was fundamentally different in each of them. Obviously, diverse people bring out different parts of ourselves. But it was also because of where we were in our stages of life.

Dan and I started out as teenagers together, full of arrogance and invincibility. We were building a life together, having children, learning who we were. As we passed from our teens to our twenties and thirties, those tasks changed. Our vision of what kind of life we wanted to build was altered. Our sense of ourselves developed and strengthened. We learned how to manage money and take care of household chores. How to be parents, however imperfectly. We developed skills and talents. Life's blows and disappointments tamed our arrogance.

In short, we grew up. But we wounded each other greatly in the process of growing up. Too greatly.

When I told Dan it was over, he was stunned, but I think he recognized the unhealthy aspects of our marriage. We had been locked in a contentious relationship for years. I had reams and reams of letters I had written explaining why I was unhappy and why I imagined he was unhappy.

When I met Perry, he and I were both accomplished adults. We knew how to take care of ourselves. We each had a world of friends, colleagues, and skills. We knew more or less what we were capable of, what we enjoyed, and what still required tweaking.

Some vast challenges lay ahead—like how we would deal with

aging and dying—but in the meantime, we focused on the pleasures in life.

Before Dan, my experience with boys was so limited. The seniors in high school flocked and sniffed around. I was flattered but totally unaware of what was expected of me. And they, I know now, were also unsure and inexperienced.

One guy, Henry, asked me to the movies, read me poetry, then jammed his tongue down my throat. I gagged. Another, Jeremy, held my hand and kissed me behind the convenience store. He later told a friend I was a bad kisser. Brian asked me for a double date. We went to the movies and, afterward, back to the basement of his house, where the other couple got busy making out. I froze.

Dan, in contrast, was a friend. He talked to me about his ideas and plans. We shared books. He was the editor of the underground newspaper. We hung out with friends, smoked dope, learned pinochle, and made Rice Krispies Treats. He passed me love notes in the hallway.

He became a performer early in his life—acting, learning magic, and staging magic shows. He had a certain charisma and could hold forth in a room full of people, entertaining and joking. He used to carry a piece of paper in his pocket with a list of punchlines. If a conversation faltered, he'd pull out his paper. After becoming a psychologist, he began testifying in court cases as an expert witness. The performances continued.

The differences between my two husbands were great at first glance.

Perry was quiet and thoughtful, didn't take up much air in a room, and listened. He was always kind, even if not always honest.

Dan was loud and impulsive, dominated the rooms, and held forth. Often cruel in the name of honesty.

When Dan and I got older, we went into therapy. We learned

not to explode in anger, to wait until we could go somewhere private to talk. I avoided the topics that would upset him. I wrote, took care of kids, paid the bills, and worked. I was familiar with this way of relating. I had grown up with it.

By the time the marriage ended, our love had disappeared into corrosive anger. The ending was no surprise to anyone except Dan. The only wonder was why it took so long.

***

In psychotherapy, people talk of repetition compulsion, which means that people are compelled to duplicate the dynamics of their pasts. This is an abstract and rather useless concept, in my estimation. People are not compelled to repeat patterns that are harmful to them; we are only going for the familiar.

In my work, victims of emotional and physical abuse often cry to me, "How could I have been with that person? How could I have stayed so long?"

Here is what I tell them: "If a person hurt you on the first date, you would be gone. But no one does that. They pull out their charming side, their funny, caring, sweet side. And sometimes that side is all you see until you're married, or often until you have children." And, I always add, "That side also truly exists. Rarely are people consistently hurtful. Their charming, sweet side is still there. We often choose to believe that is the *real* version while ignoring the other."

With Perry, as I was getting to know him, I thought, here is a grown-up. Here is a man who is aware of his feelings, knows how to manage them, and is comfortable expressing them. I believed he could ask for what he wanted.

But as I scroll back through memories, I realize that Perry wasn't so great at expressing his needs. He just wasn't volatile or angry.

At their core, my husbands were not that different.

Both were highly anxious and unsure they were "enough."

Neither was terribly self-reflective. Both tended, when feeling upset or tense, to seek a solution outside themselves. One gravitated to blaming, and the other opted to flee.

Dan's expression of this was not pleasant to live with. He criticized and found fault.

Perry's expression of this tended toward escape, a change of scenery: going to the movies, a walk by the ocean, a nap, a trip.

Perry's way was much easier to live with.

CHAPTER 16

Does Perry already have a new relationship? Or is he acting on some fantasy? My friend Ricky and I cover this ground together, often talking multiple times a day.

Ricky is the most brilliant woman I know. She is funny, honest, and irreverent. Because we both grew up in New York, we speak bluntly, sometimes impatiently. I know she believes Perry is a lying, cheating bastard—but the wonderful thing about Ricky is that she doesn't beat me over the head with it. She patiently listens as I describe our latest conversation in minute detail. She keeps listening as I ask the same questions again and again.

I'm having trouble remembering simple tasks. My muscles have clenched, making my movements jerky. I walk with my head down, checking my foot placement. My whole body hurts. I hope I am not dying of cancer. That would be the kicker!

The kids are coming this weekend, hoping to cheer me up and distract me. I tell myself this is a good thing. I am numb. I can't even cry anymore. I wish I could read. I remind myself, when I am impatient with my spinning mind, that it hasn't even been two weeks. As I organize for the kids' arrival, I try to be gentle with myself, but this process is not helped by a series of emails from Perry, one after the other.

> *Gin,*
> *I hear you asking me how could I have appeared so*
> *happy and fooled you like this for months now (or for*
> *what you worry is even a much longer time) — that*

*is, you are asking: what was and what is the reality of
our relationship?*

Gin,
*If I'm going to try to seriously date someone of a
traditional mindset who is from Vietnam with a view
toward getting married and if I want to have children, then I think I'd like to be single and available.*

I don't fume or shake when I receive this message. The shock is
passing. The reality is sinking in—and it's worse than my imaginings. My understanding of how to be in the world has been shaken
to the core. I forgave myself for choosing Dan because I was young
and naive. How will I ever forgive myself for Perry? There are not
enough years left.

I was so sure I was wise enough not to be hurt again. I thought
I was done with this kind of drama. I expected more from myself,
especially at this age, especially as a therapist. I so much do not
want to start over again, to create a new life. I was okay about
starting over in my forties after my first marriage ended. But at sixty-one? And what is this about starting over? Does it mean finding
a new love? I don't want a new love; I want a love that lasts, one
that ripens and deepens over years and years. At my age, it's not
likely that I'll find that in a do-over.

***

Later in the afternoon, I receive yet another email from Perry.

*Ann is the name of the graduate student I met at the
airport on her way to Vietnam. She's currently at
the University of Georgia. She's attending a summer*

program in New Hampshire in July.

Ann. The airport woman has a name. *Ann* conjures up a willowy blond, probably because she's in Georgia, even though, as a Vietnamese woman, she more likely has dark hair. Ann must be the American name she chose. Perry and Ann must have been emailing back and forth to arrange for her to come to New Hampshire in the summer. I wonder how long that's been in the works.

The email continues:

> *There is a strong attraction between us, and she is coming up here so that she and I can spend some time together. It may sound like several things might be said about all this - like: 'There's no fool like an old fool'; like: 'your husband is a heartless asshole who is only thinking with his dick' like: she is using me for a sham marriage, so she can stay in the U.S. after she finishes her studies.*
> *I think part of what you need and want answered is how could I give up our marriage for someone I barely know?*

He's right. There is so much I could say about this.

It's official. I've been married to a crazy man. Does that make me a crazy woman? Possibly. I will be figuring that one out for a long, long time.

Ricky calls after I forward his email. "She's so pregnant."

We dissect the timing. If he met Ann over the Christmas break and slept with her, then perhaps after he returns home, she discovers she's pregnant, likely in March. She tells him. He finally gets up the nerve to tell me in May. If this theory is true, his leaving is still devastating, but at least it explains the need for a fast divorce and the sudden urge for babies.

My kids arrive for Memorial Day weekend with a cooler of food and take over the cooking. I decide this role reversal is temporary so it's okay. My publisher, Tom, asks for an author bio, making my publishing a novel in a few weeks a bit more real. My grandson Darwin wants me to hunt dinosaurs. Margaret, from my Portsmouth writers' group, has offered to hold the book launch party.

In Boston, the house across the street from my son Zac is for sale. He's cooking up a scheme for me to be able to move there. He's gotten his father, my ex-husband, to agree to buy it with him. I can live in it and pay Dan rent until my Durham house sells. It's an unconventional idea. Or if the Durham house sells quickly, maybe I can buy the house myself. The implications and logistics are difficult to think about, but I say yes. I will have a place to land.

On Sunday, the kids and I spend the day in Portsmouth and New Castle. A day that all New Englanders welcome, seventy degrees and breezy, low humidity, trees in bloom, no clouds, all blue sky and green growth and blue sea and white sand. I feel almost normal. We spread out blankets and open the cooler. My grandson runs across the sand from the blanket to the water and back in endless loops. The water is too frigid for swimming, but there are shells, rocks, and seaweed to explore.

***

Over the fourteen years that Perry and I were together, my sons and my nephews and niece went on adventures together in various combinations. Hiking the Appalachian Trail, moving to Colorado, traveling the world, working in Guatemala, biking down the East Coast. As the mother and aunt, this was wonderful to see. We were not wealthy by some standards of American wealth, but we had privilege. I watched them navigate heartbreaks, disappointments, rejections, and successes. New loves started to make the trek to New Hampshire to be introduced to Mom (or Aunt Ginny) and Perry.

My kids and their cousins had reached the age where I was no longer an authority figure to be avoided but a person they appreciated having around. They were accepting of the parts of me that once had annoyed them (or at least were keeping quiet about it). This is one of the benefits of having children so young. It may not have been best for the kids, given that Dan and I had no idea what we were doing, but when they were in their thirties, I was only in my fifties.

With me and Perry, the kids got to see a very different model of an adult relationship. Their view of marriage was no longer limited to the loud fighting Dan and I had modeled. When Perry and I disagreed, we had conversations. We gently teased each other about our quirks. We had inside jokes. The atmosphere was calm, warm, and welcoming.

Perry did struggle with the disruptions that came from hosting this clan, but he was willing and gracious, even if depleted by the raucous energy. He handled the food shopping and often the cooking. He didn't particularly enjoy being in a crowded room with everyone talking at once, but he made sure to spend individual time with each of them, catching up on their lives.

Now, I wonder if, as the kids went off on trips, applied to graduate schools, or brought new loves to visit, Perry was jealous of these displays of youth. The kids were young and brilliant and just starting lives that stretched endlessly before them. They had strong opinions on everything and voiced them (often loudly). They might not all get what they wanted in life, but it wouldn't be for lack of trying.

I can imagine that for Perry, this crowd of young people with all their options contrasted sharply with how he felt about his own life and accomplishments. I expect he wished he had more to show for all his living. Perhaps it heightened his awareness of his age and made him restless.

During our time together, there were many weddings as this generation began to pair off. Dancing at the weddings of these "kids" with whom I'd giggled, had water fights and yelling fights, and was now seeing them in love and starting off filled me with gratitude and pride.

I loved these young adults, loved the family gatherings and staying up late talking way into the night. We often included Perry's sister and her daughters, but it became obvious that it distressed Perry. He became quiet and didn't engage in the conversations. Sharing his home and being with so many people who had claims to my time, energy, and affection exhausted him.

Over time, we worked out ways to make the visits easier for him. It was fine for him to go off to bed and have time to read. No one's feelings would be hurt. We made plans for him to go off and play tennis and take a break. I was proud we'd worked out a good rhythm.

***

When the kids and I get home from the beach at New Castle, Perry calls. This is the phone call during which he has promised to finally reveal what is going on. I'm both dreading what he is going to say and desperate to finally hear it.

I go out to the garden to talk privately while the kids cook dinner. I slide into the Adirondack chair that Perry built, clutching my wineglass. In the fading light, the trees are dark silhouettes against the indigo sky. I can hear critters rustling in the underbrush.

Perry begins by describing the traffic jam he's been stuck in, wanting, I think, to buy time, to delay.

I'm not having it. I redirect him like a traffic cop. "Tell me clearly the truth of why you're leaving. Tell me what happened. Give me the complete beginning, middle, and end. Please. Tell me all of it. Everything."

"I don't find you sexually attractive anymore," he begins.

I cut him off. I'm okay with him not mentioning that ever again. "You ended our marriage over email. Then you told me that you wanted children and wanted to find someone, and mentioned some guidance counselor at school. But then you said and told me in dribs and drabs about meeting a woman named Ann at the airport. Please tell me the truth. The whole, real truth."

Perry is silent.

I wait as darkness descends and the mosquitoes arrive. I hear the kids talking in the house and banging pots as they cook.

He finally speaks. "When Ann, the woman I met in the airport, comes up this summer, we'll see if it works. To see if we have as much of a connection as we think. And if we don't, there are women in Vietnam who need green cards."

Even in my state of shock, I'm shocked. The fact that he could even think such a thing appalls me. He's choosing women because they're economically desperate. That he could say this out loud to me, his wife, crushes me.

"I know you think I'm ridiculous," he continues. "That I'm too old for this, and no one would be attracted to me, and I shouldn't have babies at this age." His tone has turned angry. "Why did you tell me about that friend who said that urinary infections can cause dementia in the elderly?" he demands.

He's trying to distract me and change the subject. I take a sip of my wine. "Why weren't you talking to me, letting me know that our marriage was in such trouble? Why didn't you mention, at least once, about wanting children?"

"You don't listen."

"What do you mean?" I ask, caught off guard. Listening is what I do for a living.

"Like when I fucking wanted a more powerful snowblower!" he shouts. "Or the toolshed!"

"Why are you yelling at me?" I ask, bewildered. Yelling is not part of our repertoire. I don't remember even arguing over these things. I do remember that when he suggested a toolshed, I suggested we clean out the garage first. But I have no stake in low-powered snowblowers. I'm not opposed to toolsheds.

"I don't know," he mumbles.

I want to dissolve into the chair. It isn't enough. Perry was supposed to give me clarity in this phone call, not more confusion. It's a time-honored strategy for deceiving: if you don't want to answer questions, go on the attack. But I forget that at the time.

I end the call and start sobbing.

I make my way back to the house. My kids envelop me in hugs and return to the deck to sit with me. I sob some more. It feels so strange to be comforted by these men I gave birth to. But even as I let myself accept their consolation, I tell myself it is only this once. I am not ready yet, not old enough yet, for a complete role reversal.

Perry's accusation that I don't listen stings. One of the first things I learned when studying to be a therapist was to never ask *why*. We were trained to listen without judgment. *Why* might sound like it indicates curiosity, but it often feels accusatory. Why did you do that? Why did you say that?

I learned to say instead, "Can you tell me more about that?" Or, "Do you want to say more?" Or I learned to say nothing—to nod and say, "Hmm." A pause can offer people a chance to speak. The point is to listen.

I love sitting in my office, or in various dank church basements, or green-walled probation offices, and listening as people tell me their stories. I love learning about people's lives. I love hearing what they think, how they put those thoughts and feelings and actions together. I love creating the space that allows them to recognize how they feel.

People might assume therapists are like detectives, collecting pieces of information to fit together a puzzle. *Ahh—you think you are feeling that? No, no, it actually is this.* Or perhaps a game of gotcha! *I know what is really going on with you. I heard that Freudian slip.*

However, my belief is that the power and usefulness of psychotherapy is in helping people find the language to express and to share what they already know about themselves.

I do not believe I know what is best or true for anyone else. That belief has only gotten stronger as I age. But I also believe that humans sometimes suffer unnecessarily, and talking can help us express what we have been asked to keep silent.

The shrink part of me wants to listen to Perry, to hear his story. But the wife part of me wants to yell, "Why? Why, why, why?"

Perhaps it would be wise to quickly accept my changed circumstance and move on serenely, but all I want is to scream this question over and over—to stand with my hands on my hips, exuding judgment and accusation, shouting, "Why?"

CHAPTER 17

The kids leave the next morning. I am sad to see them go. It has been comforting to have company for these three days, and I know it will be a hard afternoon and evening. The house needs cleaning. I have a lot of work to do. I must get into high-functioning mode. I am so far from it.

A loving friend who also happens to be a therapist calls and tells me about a book she's reading about relationships. According to this book, people should have known all along when someone was planning to leave them. "There are always signs," she insists. "But people rarely pay attention. Not that it is your fault," she adds hastily.

This conversation agitates me. Did I ignore signs? I wander from room to room, trying to clean. I am too distracted. I have a glass of wine. After all, it's one o'clock on a holiday weekend. I open my computer and start adding the new texts and emails to my document about Perry. It is strangely calming. I can't clean up my life, but I can keep up this document.

I call another friend and tell her I should have known. She instructs me not to go down that path.

In the evening, when I'm sitting on the couch trying not to go down that path, trying to choose a movie that will offer some distraction, Perry calls.

"I'm sorry I got so testy on the phone last night. I'm not sure why I went on about the snowblower or the toolshed."

We talk for a while. Briefly, it is amicable, and I can feel a glimmer of our old connection. But I repeat my question. "What's truly happening?" I ask.

"I can't do this, Gin," he says as he listens to me begin to cry. "You're going to give me a heart attack."

He hangs up.

I should be angry, I should be furious. Perry has tremendous concern for the state of his heart and almost none for mine. I long to hold onto the relationship I thought I had with the man I thought I knew. When I'm begging Perry for answers, I'm fundamentally begging him to be the man I believed he was only a few weeks ago. I don't want him to be a ridiculous man who thinks he can find happiness with a green-card-seeking Vietnamese woman.

I take an Ativan and go to bed.

I wake up a lot. I have a brutal dream about Perry going back and forth between me and Ann. Whenever I ask him about it, he gives me a strange little half smile, a half smirk. Finally, I ask him to leave. He doesn't understand why. I end up yelling at him to go. He tries to kiss me on the way out.

***

I attend my New Hampshire writers' meeting the following day. I'd sent them some pages from my Perry Leaving Journal. One of the writers asks, "Was he always this self-involved and controlling, and hanging up on you?"

"No," I say. "I always thought he was the gentlest and kindest man I'd ever known."

I don't want to let go of the picture in my frame of the happy, wise-in-love couple.

I know that people don't suddenly change their spots. But in crisis, under severe stress, they can behave uncharacteristically. I don't know exactly what Perry's crisis is, but there has to be a *reason* for him to behave in this way. I cling to this.

Of course, we all have many sides that we don't show others, even those we are most intimate with and love the most. Generally, this is an appropriate thing. An intimate relationship would not last a minute if we shared every passing thought and feeling. *Wow, in that light, he looks old. When did that happen?* Or, *If she tells me that same work story one more time, I'm going to scream.*

But we can't carry this withholding to extremes, or we'd only have pretend relationships with pretend people. It's okay to do this with neighbors, some work colleagues, and the barista at Starbucks, but with our most intimate friends, lovers, and partners, we ache to reveal more. So, we test the waters. *If I tell you this about myself, will you still love and accept me? What if I show this ugly side, how I'm squirmy and wormy here? If I expose this shameful secret? Will you still want to be my friend, lover?* This is the difficult work of learning to love and trust another human.

It's a delicate balance. If we reveal too much, we risk loss of connection. If we reveal too little, we risk loss of self.

With Dan, I hid a great deal, but I did not think of it as concealing or lying. I simply believed I was avoiding unneeded stress over minor issues.

"Is that a new dress?"

"No, I've had this for ages."

I told myself that when it came to the important stuff, family or health or finances, I did not hide. If necessary, I fought it out with him.

But it was impossible to bring up and discuss what I hid from myself. How desperately unhappy I was, how I no longer found him funny, that his touch made my skin crawl, and I felt starved for affection.

What I can't stomach now is that perhaps Perry showed me only the parts of himself I wanted to see. That he hid from me, and maybe even from himself, everything else. That I'd been having a pretend relationship with a pretend person.

In the morning, before leaving for work, I get an email from my son Josh with an article by Anna Fels in the *New York Times* about being deceived in a marriage.

She describes people who have hidden gambling addictions or substance-abuse problems. She writes that the deceived spouse who was blindsided often reacts with humiliation, embarrassment, and shame for having been naive.

Fels goes on to state that the deceived spouse's sense of the past is disrupted. All memories are now suspect; the person often obsessively goes over past events to put a story together. "Lack of control over their destiny makes people queasy," she writes. What did I miss? What if none of my memories are true?

I latch onto one sentence: "The betrayed are usually as savvy as the rest of us."

In theory, I understand her point. I know that Perry's actions should be a reflection of Perry, not of me. Savvy, wise people are deceived in relationships as often as everyone else. Being deceived is not a character flaw.

But in practice, I do not believe this at all.

***

A day later, at the two-week mark, I wake propelled by frenetic energy. There is so much to do with the book launch, my job, and selling the house. Plus, I have to make all sorts of doctor's appointments before I lose my health insurance. I have to do all the work involved with divorce: finding a lawyer and gathering financial statements. None of this was on my calendar. I clean up a bit, make some necessary calls, write my lists, and go off to work. I'm giving a good imitation of being pretty damn functional and proud of myself. I'm realizing, slowly but surely, that I can handle this. I am putting one foot in front of the other.

On my drive to Maine, I remember seeing my shrink soon after Perry and I first met. I was terrified of ending up in another bad relationship like the one I had with Dan. I did not want to repeat that. So, I brought to my shrink all my doubts and fears. I shared Perry's and my initial relationship conflicts. I described in detail a fight we had.

"This is a man you can trust to stay with the conflict," my shrink said. "He did not disappear or run away."

When Zac calls later to check in, I tell him this story. He jokes, "Malpractice suit!"

His humor consoles me, as does the reminder that my shrink didn't see this behavior coming, either.

**

At work, on a break between clients, I see an email from Perry.

> *Obviously, I brought it on myself, but I'm having
> a pretty hellish day today thinking about what I've
> done to us and the terrible, hurtful way I did it.
> When I share about something that hurts, it isn't
> because I think you should feel bad for me;
> for me it is a starting point for communicating with
> you, by just saying what's going on with me. It might
> be a pain to listen to, but it might be my way of
> getting to talking.*

He doesn't answer when I immediately call. I don't understand what to feel about these words.

**

That night, Perry calls. He repeats that he's had a horrible day. He's in tears as he tells me he can't stop thinking about how much we had together.

I listen.

"Why don't we cancel our mediation appointment?" he says, trying to catch his breath. "Not rush to divorce."

My heart stirs. It has been leaden with aching.

"Maybe I did the wrong thing," he says.

My heart begins to skip.

"I'm thinking I—I should come home," he stammers out.

Yes! My heart leaps. I can barely breathe.

I'm full of questions. I start to speak, but Perry interrupts me. "I can't talk more now. I'll call you in the morning."

When we get off the phone, I feel elated and nearly dizzy with relief. These two-plus weeks of craziness and nightmare are over. He's coming back.

CHAPTER 18

Perry doesn't call in the morning.

There are no emails or texts waiting for me when I wake up.

If a person sincerely wants to come back, they would call, send flowers, text how sorry they are, speak a real apology. This is what I would tell a client in therapy, that the lack of a phone call tells me everything I need to know.

I make my coffee. Disappointment flattens me and slows my blood. This should've been expected, I remind my stupid, treacherous, fantasizing heart. I slip my phone into my robe pocket and take my coffee outside to the deck, shivering in the morning air. Like a little kid teasing another with a shiny toy, Perry stretched out his closed hand and slowly unfurled his fingers, but before I could see what was hiding there, he closed his fist and snapped it behind his back.

I'm furious he's given me hope—and that I let him. But still, I pull my phone out of my pocket and check again.

Do I actually want him back? This is the question I need to think about. Instead, I'm focused on waiting for him to want me again.

I decide to be preemptive. I refuse to spend this day like a teenager hanging by the phone. This is not the emotional roller coaster I want to ride. I am way too old for this.

I call Perry and leave him a voicemail. "You said you are worried about having made a mistake by leaving. Have you thought about therapy? You should take your time figuring out what you want."

I work a full day with back-to-back appointments. Zac leaves a message that he's spoken to the mortgage broker. He's putting in an offer for me on the house across the street. I am pleased. I will have a home to go to.

I also receive a brief message from Perry. He is being nominated for the best teacher of the year. That is all due to me, he says. When my last client leaves, I call him.

"I was about to write you again," he says.

Cautiously, I ask, "Where are you at emotionally?"

"I think I am making the right decision."

"To leave?" I ask.

"Yes," he answers, and I hear him begin to cry.

I stare out the window. "I'm the one who's supposed to be crying, you know," I point out. "You're supposed to be the happy one."

"I love you. We had such a good life together."

"Then why are you leaving?"

"I think it's for the best."

***

When I get home, I sit outside on the deck. I don't know what is real anymore. My fourteen-year narrative of joyful love evidently wasn't true. What else about my life isn't?

Denial and self-delusion can be useful coping strategies, but they mean my perceptions and understandings about my life are never completely accurate. They shape-shift as I age and reinterpret experiences. It's a slippery way to live, sliding around on slick ground.

It's as if I walked into my garden only to find it littered with shards of glass that used to be my sense of self. All such a mess, but I am too tired to clean it up. I stare at my glittering garden. I kick at a glass piece and watch it land in the daisies.

***

A year and a half ago, the Christmas before he went to Vietnam, we had one of our few huge fights. We were in Maine at a rental house with my kids, grandkids, niece, and nephews. We played in the snow and took walks along the winter beach and the frozen ocean. Orion's wife cooked mincemeat pies that she remembered from childhood holidays in England. Perry visited his sister on Christmas Day, returning in time for dinner. After dinner, some of us played Scrabble, and at one point, I blind traded letters with another player, a rule that Ricky and I had played with long before.

Perry exploded. "That's cheating!"

Everyone went silent, studying their tiles. No one had ever heard Perry yell. I could only remember Perry raising his voice once.

It was late. We'd all had a lot of wine.

"I should head to bed," my daughter-in-law announced, dumping her letters into the box.

We went upstairs.

"What was that about?" I asked.

"I don't know if I can take it anymore," he said.

"Take what?" My head was fuzzy, and I was upset that he'd yelled at me, especially in front of everyone.

"I wanted to stay longer at my sister's, but I had to be back for Christmas dinner."

"Why didn't you say anything?"

"I knew you'd be upset."

"I wouldn't have minded at all," I said, which was almost true. I would've been disappointed that he didn't join us, but I also would have understood.

Over the next few days, we talked. It was an uncharacteristic explosion, especially over a game. There must be more going on. I pressed him and asked questions. "Are you upset about something else? Is there more you need to talk about? Is everything okay with you? With us?"

He assured me everything was fine. He repeated that he had wanted to stay longer at his sister's and was stressed being around so many people.

But now, I go back over that fight and the discussions afterward and wonder what he didn't say. Or what I didn't hear. In my first marriage, we had too many fights. In my second marriage, perhaps we didn't have enough.

CHAPTER 19

It's been seventeen days, and later this afternoon we have our first appointment with our divorce mediator. I write a proposal for how to proceed—and for what I want. This is an act of self-preservation. Perry is acting so erratically, jumping around between moods. I'm afraid on one of his lurches, he'll file the divorce papers before we've figured out finances and I'll be left in more of a mess.

My proposal gives me all the proceeds from the sale of the house. I am the one who made the down payment, and we will likely sell at a loss anyway, so I think this is fair. I will keep all my retirement accounts; Perry will keep his. I will get whatever portion of his teacher's pension I am due under New Hampshire law. We will divide up the books and furniture. The mediator will help us file the paperwork—it's cheaper than a lawyer—and then we'll be done. I write all this up.

After I read over the document, I add a brief paragraph at the top explaining that Perry left me to find a woman to have babies with. Since he seems to cry every time we see each other, I don't want a repeat of what happened at the bank. The last thing I need is another woman who feels sorry for Perry.

As I prepare for the meeting, it occurs to me that I was the one who first raised the subject of marriage with Perry. The memory surprises me. I had always been so against the prospect of remarrying after my divorce from Dan.

***

Perry and I had been on our morning walk on Long Sands

Beach. We'd been a couple for five years and living together for two. It was a cold February day, and it dawned on me that our lives were already fully intertwined.

When he'd had chest pains a few years back and I drove him to the emergency room, we'd lied and said we were married. No one questioned it. But it made me wonder if it wouldn't be safer to formalize our relationship.

"I think we should get married," I blurted out as we walked, holding gloved hands, bundled against the winds blowing off the ocean. "That way, if anything happens to either one of us, we can be the ones the doctors share information with, and we can stay overnight in the hospital."

Perry looked at me and nodded. He pulled me in close for a long kiss.

"We don't have to do anything fancy," I said. "We could go to a justice of the peace."

"Let's have a real wedding," he declared with a grin. Perry was the romantic in our relationship. He bought presents and hid them under pillows. One time, I found a birthday gift—a necklace—hidden in the butter dish.

"We'll invite everyone we know," he continued. "We'll dance and go on a honeymoon to Europe."

I nodded, my smile perhaps a bit forced. Large weddings and honeymoons to Europe cost money.

"And we'll buy you a beautiful ring. Now, let's celebrate our engagement and go to Café Med for dinner."

We hurried to the warmth of the car and out of the cold wind.

At dinner, he wondered if he needed to wear a wedding ring. Looking back, this may have been a clue to what would happen later, a red flag, but at that moment, I asked, "Why?"

"Is it important to you?"

"Yes," I said right away. This was from the same me who refused to wear a wedding ring during her entire first marriage. At that time, I believed wedding rings signified ownership. Plus, my ring gave me a rash.

He nodded. I wonder now what that nod meant—if the fun of a wedding appealed to him, but the commitment of marriage did not.

But Perry had never seemed phobic when it came to commitment. The summer we first met, as we walked along Long Sands Beach, he announced, "Someday, I want to live in a house on the ocean with you." He squeezed my hand as we walked. Ahead of us were the bluffs. It was high tide, and the embankment on our right dropped off to the sea, covering the rocks. Clear light, cloudless blue sky, gulls screeching and diving, the road littered with the clam shells the birds dropped onto the hard surface to crack them open.

"That would be fun," I said mildly, squeezing his hand back. *Like that could ever happen,* I thought. People like us couldn't afford houses on the ocean. It was a grand romantic fantasy.

But three years later, Perry and I lived in a winter rental on the Nubble in York, Maine. It was a shabby, drafty, creaky place set high on a rock cliff overlooking the ocean and a short walk to the lighthouse. It was sublime. We watched the eiders bob in the swells from our living room. During storms, the waves crashed and sent spray up past our windows. That house showed me that fantasies could perhaps come true.

And so, I went into our wedding thinking not only about practicalities, illness, powers of attorney, an executor, but about joy.

Greg, a good friend in Boston with a huge old Victorian, offered to host the wedding. Susan from my women's group offered to organize it all. On a gorgeous day in July, among the flowers in the yard and with toasts from our families and friends, we married.

We honeymooned at the Beachmere Inn in Ogunquit, where the towels were folded into kissing swans, and rose petals were strewn on the bed. We celebrated our anniversary there every April, in the off-season, the month we met.

It was the place we'd returned to the previous month, two weeks before he left me.

***

When I get to the mediator, I hate her on sight. She has short blond hair and pale skin. Her top is beige over a cream-colored skirt. She speaks in an unnecessarily soft voice. She reminds me of white bread, which is so soft that it sticks to your teeth.

I know I am being irrational—that I shouldn't hate her. I am just resentful because I don't want to be doing this. When Perry agrees to everything I propose, he tears up. I have no idea why he's crying anymore. I want to leave fast before he really gets going.

But the mediator has one last question, one that Perry has not thought to ask. "Why," she asks in her too-soft voice, "do you want a portion of Perry's pension if you are not giving him part of your retirement accounts?"

This may be a reasonable question. In that moment, I do not see it that way. My retirement accounts are all that I have. I don't have a pension coming to me.

I immediately decide I'm finding another mediator as Perry and I walk out together.

He hugs me goodbye and then starts crying.

"Why are you always crying?" My words come out with impatience. I pull away, but part of me wonders if we will ever touch again—if this will be our last embrace. I don't know what to do. His constant crying muddles me, causes me to worry, to want to take care of him, to smack him.

Later that same evening, as the light is fading into the warm June night, Perry calls. "I just wanted to hear your voice," he says.

I close my eyes. "Tell me this," I say. "If you were unhappy and hiding it for so long, why couldn't you hide it until after my book launch? Or until the house sold?"

Silence.

"Believe me, there is nothing you can tell me now that is going to make it worse for me. It will only make it better."

Silence.

I have become obsessed with wanting facts, the straight narrative from beginning to end, the whole truth. If I hear a clear story, I won't be so confused. My grief will be transformed into something easier and less painful. How hopeful I am that simple information is the way to keep me from tumbling over the precipice. I do not want to plunge completely into despair.

"You are leaving me after fourteen years for someone you met twice?" I say. I want him to hear how insane this sounds.

"I have to go now." He hangs up.

It is dark. I hear footsteps outside. There is banging on my door. Bang. Bang. Bang. My car is in the driveway, and all the lights are on, so it's obvious I'm home. I stand where the person can't see me, but I can see if he or she goes back down the drive. I don't hear the person move. I wait. I hear footsteps, but not down the drive. This person is going around the side to the back of the house. I can't remember if I locked the back door.

I call the police.

A police car comes up the driveway. An officer gets out of the car and starts toward the house, but he stops, talks on his walkie-talkie thing, then hurries to his car and zooms back down the drive.

I call the police again, feeling foolish. The dispatcher explains that the officer was called to provide backup to another officer in the area.

The police car comes back. I answer the door, and the officer tells me they apprehended someone who admitted to knocking on doors, claiming to be working for a nonprofit organization. He didn't have any of the permits or ID he needed, so he was taken to the station.

I don't know what to make of this. Was he simply a guy trying to do good who's now been arrested because some old lady got spooked?

I am not used to being scared. I am not easily frightened. And yet, at this time, alone on the hill, anything rattles me. I am nervous going up and down the spiral stairs, anxious as I carry in wood, and hesitant to bring the garbage down the steep drive to the street. If I fall, no one will know. I remind myself to bring my cell phone everywhere, but I often forget. My fearful side startles and repulses me. I have become old.

**

In the morning, I drive to Boston. When I arrive at Orion's house, eighteen-month-old Didi runs to me, squealing, and leaps into my arms. We twirl and giggle together.

My daughter-in-law has made sticky toffee pudding, an English dessert, which I have been raving about since our trip to Cornwall, England, for their wedding. Everyone is taking such good care of me.

Hannah and Orion ask all sorts of questions, and we talk in and around playing with Didi. They are wonderful. I like what Orion has to say. "I will follow your lead here," he tells me. "If you end up angry and hating Perry, I will too. If you end up back together again and loving and forgiving him, I will too."

I marvel at my son.

Later, Zac takes me through the house he's been telling me about. This has all happened so fast it doesn't feel real, but the house is perfect. It is in Jamaica Plain, a Boston neighborhood I love. It is across the street from Zac and a mile away from Orion. Ricky lives around the corner. Greg, who hosted our wedding, lives a T stop away.

It's an old two-family built in 1890 on a dead-end street that borders a wooded section of the Forest Hills Cemetery. At the bottom of the street is a T station.

Shirley, the owner, has lived in the house her entire life; her grandfather built it. She is past eighty and moving into assisted living. "He's an idiot," she proclaims, referring to Perry. Zac must have told her my story. Then she takes me through her unit on the second and third floors. It's carpeted with pink shag, has five bedrooms, and was last updated in the 1940s. She rents out the first-floor two-bedroom unit where Zac imagines I'd live. The kitchen has a cast iron sink, a stove, and a refrigerator. There are no cabinets or counters. The bathroom has a clawfoot cast iron tub and an afterthought shower. Zac explains his idea of installing a second bathroom in Shirley's unit and renting it out. It's difficult to take all this in, but I trust Zac's wisdom. It's a great location, and anything else can be dealt with.

As I leave to drive back to New Hampshire, I get a text from Perry: *Drive safely if you're on the road. Big rain storms predicted.*

This is like a text from the olden days. Before he left.

"Who is this man?" I say out loud in the car.

That's not the relevant question anymore, I tell myself.

What do I feel? I ask.

This, I finally realize, is more important.

But I'm at a loss how to answer.

CHAPTER 20

On a bright June morning, I take my coffee and sit outside on the deck in the warm sun. It's been three weeks. I stare at a chipmunk with little black stripes on its back, skittering in and out of fissures in the boulder that the deck surrounds. It's like watching my brain. First, it runs over the rock and down toward the base, then disappears into a crevice, pops out and scoots to another crack, then runs over the top again. The creature never pauses, never stops to rest. It must be exhausted.

I hear my phone ring and go back inside. It's Zac calling to say that the offer on the house was accepted. I do not fully understand how he is working this miracle, but I am very, very grateful. Now, if I can sell this house, I will have a place to go. I have an appointment with the real estate agent at noon.

Perry has yet to ask me where I'll live. I find this more than peculiar. *Where will you live? Where are you going?* These are questions strangers ask when they hear you're moving. But my husband asks nothing.

I am so tired, I can barely stand. Pulling myself together, I open my computer and get to work on my client reports.

The real estate agent arrives, and I pour us coffee at the kitchen table while I tell her my sad story. She tells me she was married with two children and one day, her husband came home and said he wasn't into the whole having-kids-life anymore. He left, married someone else, and had a baby.

I decide there should be a new diagnosis in the DSM-V, the

manual for psychotherapists, that simply reads: MALE.

***

For the next few days, I rise too early, depressed and depleted from anxiety dreams. I dream about terrible disasters. I dream I get fired.

I tell myself to plant flowers and start cleaning out the garage. All I can actually do is take a shower.

On the day my book comes out, I force myself to go into Portsmouth to see it in the store. RiverRun is a small independent bookstore that has struggled to survive during all the years I've lived in New Hampshire. The book-reading people in Portsmouth rallied and helped Tom, the owner, move from higher-rent storefronts to lower-rent ones. Tom decided to branch out into publishing and created this contest for novelists.

At the store, Tom beams as he hands over my book. I stroke the cover. Here it is, the culmination of over twenty years of work and dreams. I want to feel elated and ecstatic. But I feel ... nothing. I've lost my range of feelings. I'm limited to sadness and anger, but mostly, I'm numb.

I smile. I nod. I mumble my thanks and say something about needing to get to an appointment. I hope and pray I do not seem rude as I all but run to my car.

My mother would be proud of me for writing a book. She was a voracious reader. She would often come home with a new book she thought I'd like or pick one off the shelf in the living room for me. This love of reading was our connection.

Reading has saved my life. Actually, *reading* is a mischaracterization. I inhale books. I am lost without reading. I read novels and nonfiction, history, essay collections, memoirs, and books on nature and neuroscience. Anything and everything. And this is all due to my mother.

My mother was brilliant but unable to attend college because she had to work and care for her own mother. She frequented speakeasies and smoked cigarettes during Prohibition in New York City. She worked as a secretary. She slept with my father before they were married. She admired Katherine Hepburn. She wanted to be a flapper so cut her hair short. She came of age in an era of films about classy broads with smart mouths.

She met my Italian father, also smart, also fatherless, also penniless, in one of those speakeasies. My father had two brothers and two sisters and a mother who ran the show. All in Italian.

My maternal grandmother, a Scot, hated my father. He was a low-life Sicilian, perhaps attached to the Mafia, and a Catholic to boot.

My mother married him anyway.

I know little about the early years of their marriage, except that all the Italian relatives lived close together in Brooklyn. When my uncles, Tony and Sam, got called up to fight in WWII, Aunt Lee, Aunt Mary, and my mother moved in with my nonna to be together while the men were at war. Because my father was a fireman, he was exempt during the first years of the draft, but eventually, he was called up as well.

My maternal grandmother also lived with them for a short time in Brooklyn. Apparently, she tried to push my mother out of a second-story window. My mother was hanging laundry on the pully line attached to the apartment house across the way. Even as an adult, I never heard a clear explanation as to why; perhaps it was alcohol-related dementia. After this, my father insisted that my grandmother be put in a nursing home. My mother said that every time she visited, my grandmother begged her to take her out.

"Never," my mother would say to me adamantly, "have just one child." My mother must have carried guilt and grief alone for years.

After the war, my parents moved out to Long Island. This was a huge deal. The rest of the Italian family also left Brooklyn, but they moved to Queens, within walking distance of each other. Our family lived a whole car ride away. Later, when my cousins visited, they called it "going to the country."

My parents furnished their house with secondhand couches and chairs, which my mother would re-slipcover over the years. She rarely bought anything new. With books and plants, she created a warm, inviting home.

In the 1950s, when television arrived, I learned from the commercials that women took great pleasure in cleaning soap scum from bathtubs and removing ring-around-the-collar, and making sure they stayed attractive for their working husbands.

Without making speeches or pronouncements, my mother tried to counter those messages. She introduced me to Margaret Mead, the anthropologist, who spoke at the local Unitarian church to show me women could be thinkers.

She introduced me to Margaret Sutton, the author of the Judy Bolton Mystery Series, to show me that women could be writers.

When my father dismissed his sisters as foolish and not very bright, my mother quietly contradicted him, insisting that Aunt Mary and Aunt Lee were both smart.

Nurturing and taking joy in small children was not my mother's strength. But she instilled in me my love for reading and books. She showed me that women could be brilliant and bold. For that, I am grateful.

***

At home, clutching my copy of my first published novel, I sit in the beige chair with the ottoman that used to be "Perry's chair." I again run my hand over the cover, waiting for the appropriate feelings of joy and pride. Nothing.

I open my computer, decide to get some work done, and see this email from a friend.

> *Your life IS great!!! Your family loves you! Your friends love you! Your clients love you! AND YOUR BOOK IS ON AMAZON! YEAH!!!!!!! Your life is amazing! Now, how do we get you to feel happy before you actually are happy? What would a therapist tell you if Perry had died in an avalanche? (instead of snow, he is buried under a ton of stupid.) By the way, what color vibrator should you get?*

I laugh. It feels good.

Friends and family have been saving my life. My women's group is in constant contact. My writer friends are making sure my accomplishment of publishing does not get lost in grief. Ricky designed Evites to the launch and read many of my drafts for the reading. Margaret is organizing the launch party for after the reading. Bett has been reading proofs and conferring with the publisher. Julie has designed my website. My colleagues at work are jumping in every way possible to help me out. My bosses are arranging work for me out of the Boston offices after I move.

I feel like the luckiest and most ill-fated woman alive.

CHAPTER 21

A few days before my book launch, five weeks after Perry left, I head to the eye doctor to pick out new glasses. I want a new look. Perhaps, I think wryly, new glasses will give me a new perspective.

A pleasant young man shows me frames with wireless rims, brown ovals, and black squares at the small shop on Daniel Street in Portsmouth. They are age-appropriate frames but muted and depressing. I don't like anything.

I look up from the sea of bland. "I just published a book, and I'm doing a reading over at RiverRun Bookstore, and my husband left me a month ago to make babies with a new woman. I need frames that say beautiful, brilliant, and badass."

Everyone in the shop goes silent. They stare at me.

I shrug apologetically.

A young woman of about eighteen who was organizing files strides over. She reaches for a pair of large, bright multicolored frames, with turquoise the dominant shade, unlike anything I've previously worn.

"How about these?" she suggests.

They are loud. They are colorful. They are bold.

"Perfect," I say.

***

When I get home, the real estate agent texts that there is an offer on the house.

A few minutes later, Perry texts to tell me he's playing tennis in Portsmouth. I have no idea what these updates on his activities and whereabouts signify. He has a way of texting precisely when glimpses of my possible new life are coming into focus.

I hope he has a heart attack.

I choose not to reply.

***

The following day, I wake up too early. Three-thirty, to be precise. I am bleary and unsettled. It's too early for coffee and too late for wine. I compromise, have half a glass of wine, and crawl into bed with the movie *Crazy, Stupid, Love.* In the first scene, a middle-aged husband (Steve Carell) is told by his wife (Julianne Moore) that she wants a divorce. He jumps out of the moving car and moves out that evening. The rest of the movie concerns the question of how much we should fight for our soulmates. I hate the word *soulmates.* It implies cosmic destiny, and I don't believe in that at this point in my life.

But the movie has me questioning again if I should be fighting for my marriage instead of wallowing about being left. I believe lifelong love comes from the choices we make. There's the choice to not behave in ways that hurt our loves. The choice to apologize when we do hurt them. The choice to confront ourselves when we prefer to ignore how we hurt our loves, intentionally or unintentionally. The choice to learn how our behaviors can cause hurt even when we don't mean to or understand why. The choice to do the work of learning about another human. Maybe I'm making the wrong choice.

As the sun comes up, it's now late enough for coffee. I try to read the offer on the house. It's difficult to understand. I can't do this. I can't sell this house. My hands tremble, making the pages waver. I think I will be sick. I can't do this. I take a deep breath and hold it for a five count. Of course, I can do this—because I have no choice—but really? I can't do this. I knew when we first decided to put the house up for sale that I would be so sad to leave the trees, the gardens, the birds, and the reading by the wood stove. I knew that! But I thought we would be undertaking another adventure in our lives. Together.

All gone. All over. Oh, God, I don't want to be doing this.

It was here, in my study high among the trees, that I pulled out the drafts of the novel I'd carted around for years. I found the writers' group in Portsmouth that helped those drafts become a book. I don't want to leave this house with the gardens and the Adirondack chairs that Perry built, where I have coffee in the morning sun. I don't want to leave the Seacoast and my New Hampshire friends. I don't want my life with Perry, our love, to vanish, poof, a wisp of smoke dissolving in the air until it might never have existed at all.

When my father left my mother after thirty-five years of marriage, my mother often said, "Why didn't he leave ten years ago, when I was forty-five instead of fifty-five, so I could have made another life?"

From my vantage point of eighteen, that didn't seem like a big difference. From my vantage point of sixty-one, I get it. What if I'm destined to dry up, rattling in empty spaces, dithering about if I should paint a wall blue or white, watching people's eyes slide away because they pity me and my lonely, boring life. What if I am too old to make a different life? Damn, I want a new vision of growing old. I want to see myself with the wind in my hair, the sun at my back, and a huge shit-eating grin on my face as I turn forward, knowing I'm facing the final installment of my life and being open to whatever might happen from here to there. I want a new path.

***

I've spent my career helping people unpack what they experienced in childhood and how it impacted their behaviors and lives later on—not as an excuse but as an explanation. A favorite story I tell is of a woman cooking roast beef. Before she places the meat in the roasting pan, she always hacks off a hunk.

"Why do you do that?" asks her daughter.

"It was how my mother did it."

"Why?" asks her daughter.

"I don't know," says the woman. She calls her mother and asks, "Why did you always hack off a chunk before you put the meat in the pan?"

Her mother informs her, "Because the roasting pan I had was too small."

I wish I could go to my mother and ask her questions like this.

***

After my father left, my mother moved to Vermont to live in the cabin my parents had used as a vacation place. It was tiny: one large room divided by the stairs to the attic dormer. One side was the kitchen area, and the other was the living room area. Out back was a large two-story barn. A wraparound deck looked over the rolling field down to the pond. Black-eyed Susans, orange daylilies, white daisies, and baby's breath bloomed in the grass.

"Can you believe it?" my mother said more than once. "A girl from Brooklyn living up here?" And she'd wave her arm at the expanse of trees, fields, and streams.

At the time, it seemed sad to me—tossed and tumbled with no agency, ending up alone on a dirt road. But possibly, my mother was telling me she liked it.

Every Monday, my mother drove to the library in Montpelier and took out piles of books. She told me that the librarian saved her the new releases, and then she would ask my mother for her reviews the following week. They'd chat about the books, and my mother would leave with a new book pile. When she got home, she'd sit on the deck, a book in her lap, apple and cheese slices on a plate within reach, and watch the shadows float over the lawn from the clouds.

***

Dan and I would pile the three kids in the car for one week every summer and visit my mother in Vermont. My brothers and their kids would join us. It was a week of roaming the woods, lighting sparklers, and barbecuing chicken. Also, alcohol and cigarettes. A lot of alcohol and cigarettes.

My mother was a nasty drunk. Her favorite drink was a vodka martini—hold the vermouth and the olives. That's a great deal of vodka. After one drink, she'd complain about the wet clothes drying in the field or toys strewn in front of the barn. After two, she'd berate the grandkids about a freezer door left open or unwashed dishes in the sink, detailing the character flaws these mistakes indicated. After three, she'd start in on her adult children. I'd insist she take a walk if she got too mean. Later, I told her I would not visit if she drank while we were there.

***

When I was thirty-two and my mother was sixty-eight, she was diagnosed with lung cancer. She immediately tried to quit smoking.

"Mom, don't worry about quitting. It's a bit too late," I said.

I accompanied her to doctor appointments and scary procedures, leaving my kids and Dan behind, traveling from Boston to Burlington, Vermont, not wanting her to be alone.

Six weeks after her diagnosis, my mother was in the hospital in Vermont, sick with sepsis. Again, I drove up from Boston.

The doctor told her they could prolong her life for another few weeks, possibly a month.

When he left, my mother grabbed my arm and pulled me close. "I'm done. Make this dying happen."

I remember this command as a hiss.

I spoke with my oldest brother, Ken, and his sons in the waiting room. We called our brother John and told him to hurry from Connecticut.

My mother told the doctor that she was ready to die. "Give me the pill," she announced.

"There is no pill," he said, "but we will keep you comfortable."

In 1985, this meant the doctor agreed to give her enough morphine to suppress breathing, and he agreed to stop all treatments except for pain relief.

When John arrived, my mother called us individually to her room to say goodbye.

I pulled my chair close to the bed and held her hand.

"I know I wasn't the best mother."

I immediately took my hand away from hers, reaching to give her water. Annoyance flashed. *What could I say to that?*

Should I have nodded and said that I agreed? Should I have protested and told her she was the best? Her statement required an entire conversation, many conversations, and there was no longer time.

I took her hand again and told her I loved her—that much was true. She did not say it back. Words of affection never came easily to her.

I don't know what she said to my brothers, but when she was finished, she called me back into the room and again clutched my arm. "There is a box underneath the stairs in my cabin. A metal box. It will have all the papers you need." My mother and I had never spoken of end-of-life details. I nodded.

Then she said, "Get the doctor, tell him I'm ready."

Ken's sons had tears streaming down their faces, and they didn't bother to wipe them.

The doctor repeated to her that they could treat the sepsis, and she could be well enough to leave the hospital at least for a few weeks. Maybe even months.

"No," she said. "I don't want to go in and out of the hospital for weeks."

And so the doctor gave her enough morphine to "keep her comfortable." And we all stayed by her side. She slipped in and out of consciousness. The nurse showed me how to use a swab to moisten her lips. The last thing she said was, "Who knew you would turn into such a good nurse?"

After she died, we found the metal box under the stairs in her cabin. Everything we needed to deal with her death was in there and carefully filed.

**

I didn't know at the time, but this was the role I would also take on for my father, for John, and for Ken. For all of them, I faced the task of ushering them out. At least I won't face this with Perry

CHAPTER 22

Every winter, my father turned our small backyard into an ice skating rink. He constructed it with two-by-fours, sheet plastic, and three inches of water. As soon as the temperature dropped and the water froze, we'd skate. At my mother's funeral, my cousin Frank spoke about how some of his best childhood memories involved my mother hosting skating parties. Frank described how exciting it was to skate at night under the floodlights, and how my mother would serve hot chocolate with big marshmallows.

But what I remembered was her fury. She would fret and complain about the work and the imposition. Her rage barely contained, she'd slap mugs onto a tray and yell if I didn't help quickly enough. It was a behind-the-scenes secret between us as she put on a good show.

My cousin saw what was in the frame: the pretty picture. I saw what was outside of it: the angry reality.

When my mother died, I was numb for weeks with the pain of her death. And numb for months with the pain of her life. And numb for years with the pain of our fraught relationship. I wore her clothes. I put her photo on our picture board. I kept her colored glass bottles and garden clippers.

My older brothers might not have had the language to talk about my mother, but they did their best to shield me, a baby born to a woman with no language to explain her rages.

Ken graduated from high school in 1958, the same year I graduated from kindergarten. At that time, I thought the party held in the backyard among the zinnias and marigolds was for me, and I twirled in a skirt that stood out sideways because of the crinoline, a stiffened scratchy material. Ken would be the first of the entire extended family to graduate college, but I did not want him to go away. I cried over his departure. On every return visit, he brought me a stuffed animal.

When I was six, my brother John discovered me in my bedroom making a map of an imaginary town for my stuffed animals. Using many colored crayons, I drew it directly on the wood floor. The bunny with a vest and glasses was the mayor.

These animals from Ken, the bossy rabbit mayor, the ferocious mouse, and the silly tiger, populated the town I was creating when John found me. I must have looked frightened when he appeared in my doorway. I remember him saying everything was okay and it was a beautiful drawing, but we would need to clean it all up before Mom saw it. He got the rags and Windex. He sank to his knees and scrubbed.

John taught me to dance in our living room. He put a record on the turntable, placed my feet on his toes, and taught me to cha-cha. Stepping and swirling, laughing with delight and anticipation, I imagined myself at a high school dance. Of course, there was no such thing as dancing the cha-cha when it was my turn for high school ten years later.

In adulthood, our nine-year age difference shrank to nothing. John married and had three kids in his late twenties. I married and had my kids early, so our children were around the same age. Although we never lived in the same city, we traveled to spend holidays, vacations, and a week every summer together. Our kids loved these times and became especially close.

I have vivid memories of John and me on the beach in Wellfleet, Massachusetts, talking and laughing as our kids—six of them—ran the beach, dug in the sand, played elaborate fantasy games, and built cities out of driftwood. Our blankets lay spread, piled with sweatshirts, suntan lotion, and newspapers. We'd packed two coolers full of peanut butter sandwiches, beer, juice, peaches, and napkins. This was luxuriousness of the highest order. Later, we piled the kids into the car and drove to Provincetown for dinner. We drove along the dunes through the late sunlight, with the Beach Boys playing at full volume, the kids giddy from surprise at such carefree adults. Every night that week, we had root beer floats on the pier with the tar smell, the fishing boats, and the moon making its strong light shadow on the water.

***

Four years later, in the summer of 1987, John died of AIDS. He was forty-three.

That previous year, he'd been very ill, in and out of hospitals with mysterious symptoms. None of the doctors suspected AIDS or even considered it. The virus itself had only recently been discovered. The scientific community didn't yet have a universally agreed upon name for it, sometimes calling it GRID or ARC. Although researchers had developed a test for months, not one doctor thought of using it. After all, John was married to a woman; professional, white, upper-middle-class; the father of three children. This equaled *not gay*. Not at risk.

My brother, sick and afraid, talked about dying. No one in the family took that seriously.

"John," I said finally, "if you are really sick enough to die, I promise we'll give you a good death. We'll all be here, surrounding you in love."

It didn't quite work out that way.

***

We gave each other a great gift, John and I. We held ourselves up to scrutiny, putting the mirror in the merciless sunshine, and we liked what we saw reflected back.

How many people in our lives can do that for us? Not many. Not so many that we can afford to lose one without a great shattering pain.

After twenty-seven years, I still miss him. I often tell clients consumed with grief that our relationships don't end when a person dies. I imagine how much fun it would be for John and me to hang out with our grandkids, gossip and worry about our adult children, compare our latest diet or exercise regimen, and obsess over politics together.

Our separation started before his actual death. We had different places in the script. "You don't understand," he said to me. "You have no idea what this feels like."

I nodded. He was dying. I was surviving. We could hold hands. But there were precious few words to throw across that chasm.

***

I remember staring at a chip in the terra cotta tile on the kitchen floor, holding the phone as John told me he had AIDS. Pasta water heated on the stove and the kids were at the table doing homework. The sun spotlighted the tulips and daffodils in a vase on the old varnished telephone-cable spool we used as a coffee table.

I remember this the way my parents stated precisely where they were when Pearl Harbor was bombed, the way I remember my fifth-grade teacher's face when she got the news that President John F. Kennedy had been shot, and later the way our children would remember 9/11. The freezing of time.

"Eighteen months' life expectancy," John said over the phone.

"Yes," I said.

"Death 100 percent."

"Yes," I said again. *No* was what I wanted to say. But I said *yes* because I wanted him to know I would be strong for him.

"Don't tell anyone," he said next.

This I didn't expect. "Why not?"

"We have to protect the kids." His oldest was fifteen, and the twins were twelve. "They can't know. The town can't know. We're not telling anyone."

I paused. "What about Dad? And Ken?"

"Well, yes, Dad, and yes, Ken. And you can tell Dan. But there it stops. Promise me you won't tell anyone else."

"You will not go through this alone," I said, fully believing the words as I spoke them.

***

AIDS hit the media in a big way in the '80s. In some little town in Florida, mosquitoes were suspected of spreading the virus. An article appeared about the possibility of bedbugs in Africa carrying it. Children with AIDS were being hounded out of school systems. Other experts stressed how difficult it was to catch AIDS from casual contact. Fear, they said, shouldn't take over.

But it did.

Dan was terrified and didn't want our kids to be around John or their cousins. He didn't want me to visit.

"Your fears are irrational," I screamed. "My brother's dying, and I will not abandon him."

"What if they're not irrational? What if I'm right?" Dan asked, panicked. "They thought the blood supply was safe until they found out otherwise."

Over months, Dan and I fought it out while I visited John alone. The cousins, my children and John's, were hurt and confused about not being together. Finally, Dan and I agreed that in order for all of us to visit, we would tell our children so they would know not to share toothbrushes or eating utensils. We told them they must keep the secret of their uncle dying of AIDS from their cousins, his children. And they did. Even my youngest, who was only six. I cannot imagine the burden this placed on them.

Recently, when I asked Orion, who was twelve at the time, what he remembered, he said, "I remember you telling us that we must keep it all secret. I remember you telling us that Uncle John and Aunt Louise had told the cousins that he had blood cancer. I also remember asking you what to say if my cousins asked us about it. You told us we still couldn't tell. I remember saying, 'So, you're asking us to lie?' And you said, 'Yes.'"

Lies separate us. These cousins were close. They still are. But they all live with knowing they once betrayed and were betrayed by each other.

During John's final days, he asked me to look after his children, a request I found mildly insulting. "You think I wouldn't?" I asked.

"They love you so much," he said. "Please."

"Of course," I said.

I thought of us as close, incredibly close, yet we never discussed how he got AIDS. I have my theory. I believe John was closeted. He told his wife that when they were separated, he had sex with a call girl, but I suspect this was a cover story. He came of age in the 1950s when being closeted was common and often necessary. Perhaps he was okay with this and comfortable with himself. Maybe he was terribly ashamed, or maybe merely private. I will never know.

Whatever his reasons, he kept a huge part of himself separate and secret from many people, including me. Does that negate the intimacy of our relationship? Not for me. After all, I didn't discuss *my* sex life with my brother. But living with secrets is difficult and lonely. I wish he didn't have to die lonely.

The night before he died, John asked me, "Is it okay if I stop trying to live? I've tried so hard." I nodded, unable to speak, and held his hand.

***

Over many years, my kids and my brothers' kids have maintained our tradition of frequent family gatherings. It's been thirty-two years since John died. These gatherings still cause me to miss my brother with shocking intensity.

This past April, John's youngest son, Todd, and his family visited from Vermont. We lounged in my living room, joking around. We'd had some wine and smoked some dope, relaxing after a long day of wrangling little kids on vacation.

"I'm forty-four," Todd said, apropos of nothing. "I'm older than my father was when he died. It's sad."

I nodded, feeling woozy from the wine.

"But what makes me feel worse is how everyone lied to me." He looked at his cousins. "Even you. You guys all knew and never told us. Everyone kept it a secret."

What shocked me at that moment wasn't what Todd said; it was that it took so long for someone to say it. Over the past three decades, I don't remember any of John's children ever talking to me about this aspect of their father's death. What did it feel like to be lied to by their family? By me? I had never asked them. I had certainly never apologized for it.

At the time, I rationalized it by telling myself it wasn't my call. John's wife, Louise, was intent on keeping it a secret out of fear of people's reaction. Cancer, not AIDS, was listed as the cause of death in the *New York Times* obituary.

About a year after John's death, the AIDS quilt was coming to Boston. Friends, family, and lovers would gather together and make an individual three-by-six-foot panel commemorating the life of someone who had died of AIDS. It was both a memorial and a visual to help people understand the devastating impact of the disease.

I wanted our family to create a panel. I spoke to Louise. This could be a way of telling the kids and talking about John's life. She wasn't ready. I wrote a piece about John and his death and sent it off to a literary magazine. I changed all the names. I never expected it to be accepted, but it was, and I told Louise. She was furious. When it was due to be published, two years after John's death, she brought the kids to a therapist and told them their father had died of AIDS.

Families keep secrets for all sorts of reasons, but mostly because they don't know what else to do. Even now, I'm not sure what I should have done differently while John was dying. But who we are actually protecting with these secrets and lies is up for grabs.

CHAPTER 23

It's been six weeks since Perry left, and my book launch is in four days. After work, I reach for my book, turning it over, stroking the cover, rereading the blurb on the back. I'm trying to focus on picking a good section to read for my author event when Perry calls.

"I just got done with tennis," he begins.

Weeks ago, when we were still together, this would have been the start of a conversation about whether I'd eaten and if I wanted him to pick up takeout Thai food. We loved pad thai and chicken satay. Sometimes, we'd add spring rolls. I would have asked about the game, and he would've told me that they played extra sets, or maybe complained about how annoying it was to have Bill as his partner. Now, I have no idea what to say or why he is calling, so I say nothing.

"I was driving through Portsmouth, past the library on my way home, and all I could think about was you."

I close my book. I'm hating my traitorous heart, which is beating faster. It has gotten dark, and I can see my reflection in the black windows. I look calm.

"I'm having lots of doubts and regrets about leaving," he continues.

"Oh?" I say, willing my heart to slow down, knowing we've done this dance before.

"We had such a good life together."

"Yes. We did." I'm measuring hope. He doesn't say anything.

I lose patience. I can't help myself. "What exactly are you

saying?"

"I don't know," he says, and I can hear him crying.

"Let me know when you figure it out." I hang up.

***

In the morning, sitting in bed with my coffee, I again try to decide which section of my book I will use for the book launch. My concentration keeps slipping.

What does Perry mean when he expresses having regrets? I don't want to consider the question, but trying to block it out doesn't work. I force my attention back to the task at hand. The reading is in only three days.

Writing and reading have always been my world. My mother was not pleased to have my friends over after school to play, so when I wasn't in school, I spent a lot of time alone. Before I could read, I told stories in my room about my stuffed animals' town. As I got older, I wrote stories and poems on a little corner desk, where I also sometimes did homework.

Later, I would write in journals. By the time I was in high school, I always carried a notebook with me and wrote in diners and soda shops.

Writing soothed me. I never dreamed I could become a real writer, a published writer. A writer of books.

And now, at sixty-one, I am.

But my brain is not behaving. Instead of trying to pick something for the reading, I keep wondering if this is the time Perry will truly ask to come back. I fantasize about how I'll respond. I'm angry just thinking about it, the way a parent worries and agonizes over a lost child, and later, when they're found, the poor stray is greeted with a torrent of rage born of abject fear.

But I'd rather feel anger that he's back instead of this continual hope and then the despair all over again when the hope is dashed.

Of course, in the rom-com movie world, love triumphs over all these messy feelings of anger and recrimination.

I go back to concentrating on the beginning of the book. I open my computer to the novel in its Word document and start editing.

Right on cue, the phone rings. It's Perry. I let it ring a few times before I pick up.

"Hi." My voice is sharp.

"Hi."

He does not say anything else. I wait. The silence elongates, and I know this is not the call when he declares that he wants to return to me. The silence between us is heavy.

Finally, he blurts, "I think leaving is the right decision for me."

I hang up on him, slide off the bed, and walk laps from the kitchen to the living room and back. No matter if he wants to return or he doesn't, I can't handle his wavering, his indecision, his ambivalence. It's savage.

When marriages end, we lose the planned future together. I get that. I can make a new life, even if I don't want to. What I can't figure out is my old life. I can't put together the Perry I knew with this new man. It truly doesn't compute.

CHAPTER 24

On the morning of my author event, I wake with my head swimming. I should be thinking about my reading, but all I can think about are house questions and lawyer questions. If I buy the house in Boston before the divorce is final, does that mean Perry owns part of it? What are the tax implications if I take money from my 401(k) for the down payment?

The kids all descended on me yesterday, and I can hear Orion playing with his daughter, Didi. I get out of bed.

I will call the lawyer on Monday. And my accountant.

Friends, family, and colleagues are traveling here from Maine, Boston, western Massachusetts, and Vermont. I know they are coming to support and celebrate me, but it feels more like a wake. In one month, I will be leaving this New Hampshire life.

We play outside with the babies on this easy, lazy morning, and then I dress and drive to the Lamprey River to practice my reading one more time in the car.

The bookstore is on Fleet Street, a block from Market Square, and today, the store is packed, the bookshelves are pushed to the sides, and folding chairs fill the space.

I am not a natural public speaker. So, I practiced and practiced.

I thank my family. I thank Tom. I thank my women's group. I thank everyone who has played a part in creating this moment. And I begin to read.

I make it through the reading. All that practicing and my damn voice still wavered, and I thought I would faint. But the audience laughed in all the right places. Everyone said the reading went well, and even people I didn't know asked to get their books signed. One of Perry's colleagues comes up to me and says, "I will never understand love. Why would he leave such a dynamic woman?" I force a smile and shrug, wondering if that was a compliment, wondering if I should say thank you. But I refuse to let Perry's absence ruin this moment.

Afterward, everyone goes to Margaret's for the party. The house is in New Castle on the mouth of the Piscataqua River. People spill out from the living room to the deck overlooking the harbor and the lawn bordering the shore. I give a little speech. Others make toasts, saying how much they love the book and love me.

It is all good, in an out-of-body experience sort of way. I, too, can put on a good show.

The next day, after everyone leaves, I crawl back to bed and curl up with my pillows. My brain is dull, and my muscles are depleted. I press a pillow against the pain in my solar plexus. Too much. All too much. I'm falling apart. Again.

It's been less than two months, I sternly remind myself. I am allowed to fall apart.

My phone buzzes. It's a text from Perry telling me he'll be at the library until 2 p.m. and then will be playing tennis in Portsmouth.

I text back: *DON'T CALL OR TEXT OR EMAIL ME — unless it is about the BUSINESS of ending this marriage.*

I turn off my phone and return to curling up with my pillows.

***

Grief-land is its own territory. It's lonely and filled with steep, treacherous rocky mountain paths, sticky swampland, and lots of mosquitoes and black flies. It rains often. A solid downpour, or it's generally cloudy. Sometimes, it gets cold and sleety. There are no caves to crawl into where you can light a fire and get warm. There is no place to sleep. One must keep trudging and trudging. Occasionally, you might meet another person in this land, but they don't speak the same language, even if they're in the mood to speak and often they aren't. Our heads are down, watching our feet as we plod along.

Because just over there, maybe over the next rise or possibly the one after that, it is sunny with cool breezes that blow away the flies and mosquitoes. There are hot boulders to lean against for warmth. There are people who smile and take your hand and help you over the rough patches, hug you and feed you soup, and tell you it will be okay. You will be okay.

Everyone is dragged into Grief-land at some point; no one enters willingly.

By the time we're in our sixties, most of us have spent time in Grief-land.

I have. Which means I trust that the sunny place over the rise is truly there, and all I have to do is keep walking.

But this time around, I haven't even entered Grief-land yet. I am in some anteroom that I name Howl-land. A long wail of repeated questions and self-doubt hurled into the dark. What did I miss? What did I do wrong? What happened? And overwhelming shame.

Would this heartache be any different if he had died? If I were a widow instead of a divorcée? I would still be grieving the loss of our future together. But his untruthfulness means I'm also grieving the past, not knowing what memories are real.

I decide it would have been better if he had died. The result would be the same—he would be gone. But I would be the grieving widow with all my memories intact. I wouldn't have to deal with ambiguity or his tears.

If I had woken to find Perry dead on the floor, I would be getting a different kind of sympathy from people. But I would also be presenting a different kind of grief. It would be okay for me to tear up; it would be okay to talk about our beautiful life and how much I miss him. I could sink into the grief of it all in front of people, with people. I wouldn't have to present as so goddamn strong. I wouldn't have to try to look okay.

It's the situation of having been left that causes people to stare at the space behind my left ear, dodging eye contact. No one wants to ask too much. People don't know what to say when they hear the news. "So sorry for your loss, he was such a wonderful man" doesn't quite cut it when your husband has left you for a younger woman. I am avoided until people can ascertain that I won't spew volcanic rage or crumple into a tissue bog. So, I am in the position of presenting as cheerful, pretending that I'm okay and all is well.

I have been to Grief-land many times already, and I've learned to make friends with ghosts. I am familiar with loving dead people. I talk about them.

When alone, I talk *to* them. I obsess. I accuse. I apologize. I blame. I beg forgiveness. I write. My joints ache. I cry more tears than I ever thought possible. I examine past conversations. I parse phrases. I spend inordinate amounts of time on what could have been, if only, and why.

But I never call the ghosts' cell phones repeatedly like I do with Perry.

CHAPTER 25

During the three weeks I have to pack and get out of the house, I want to say Perry is useless but that wouldn't be true. He picks up packing cartons, packing tape, and markers from U-Haul and drops them off. He makes frequent trips to the town dump. I both want him around and don't want him around. I am grateful to have a legitimate excuse to see him, but also enraged that I must see him.

I spend the next few weeks in a blur of boxes and packing paper, feeling like superwoman with a hole in her heart. I realize I'm slightly manic, with tremendous bursts of activity that border on frantic. I need to get out of this house, need to get out of New Hampshire, need to get back to Boston. This weird energy is better than lying prone and melting into the couch, but I can't sense the ground under my feet. I keep tripping on rocks and roots and sudden dips in the soil.

***

Friends step in and pack my kitchen. My son Josh arrives for the weekend from New York and cleans and packs up the attic, carrying box after box down the spiral stairs.

As I pack, I elaborate on versions of stories that might fit with the man I thought I knew and explain both his abrupt departure and his constant weeping about it.

In one of my stories, Perry went to Vietnam, had a fling with Ann, and fell in love. I can picture how it could have happened. Past-his-prime Perry, far from home, off on an adventure, engages in innocuous flirting with a young, attractive woman. I imagine when flirting progresses to sex, he thinks: *What's the harm? No one will ever know.* The story breaks down a bit here because I *do* know, and he's talking marriage and babies. I can't figure out how that could have happened in only one week away.

In my friend Ricky's version, he has a fling with Ann, and she calls to tell him she's pregnant. This explains the never-before-mentioned urge for babies, the need for a quick divorce, and his use of the expression that he's "doing the right thing."

The only problem with these theories is that he continues to deny any sexual contact with Ann. He's sticking to "only a kiss."

Another theory is that he's had many affairs throughout our marriage and I never knew. This one is brutal and upends my whole story of our happy marriage.

***

Stories that make me feel better:

He went crazy because of turning sixty.

He got Ann pregnant and needs to "do the right thing."

He has early-onset dementia.

Stories that make me feel worse:

He's been miserable and has wanted out for a long time, but I had no idea.

He's cheated for a brief time.

He's cheated throughout our marriage.

He fell out of love. With me.

It doesn't matter which theory is true. He still wants a divorce. He will still be gone from my life. I still have to pack. So, I choose the theory that is the least painful and easiest for me to accept: that his fears about aging hit a crescendo when he turned sixty and made him nutty. Or he has a touch of dementia.

I'll worry about the truth later.

There is something to be said for denial, dissociation,

compartmentalization. I have accomplished a great deal while bleeding. I have moved quickly. In less than two months, I've managed to sell our house, buy another, launch my book, and begin to transfer my work life to Boston. But my feelings don't change that fast. I know from my work that while our rational minds can be in one place, our feelings can be in another.

"I'm still betting he'll be crawling home by November, or at least by March," says a friend who's dropped off brownies for packing energy. "I mean, who could leave *you*?"

I laugh, hug her, and thank her for the brownies. A part of me also believes this. Maybe that's why I'm watching rom-coms instead of disaster movies. I'm waiting for the happy ending.

***

The most difficult part of packing for a move is all the decision-making.

I try to sort out what I should take, what I should throw out, what I should donate. Making these decisions is impossible.

"Take it all," my kids say, "and figure it out after you get to your new place." I know I will regret this at the other end, but it does make packing go much faster.

I need Perry's input with dividing the books and cleaning out the garage. He brought a lot of stuff from his previous lives. I almost chuck it all. He has not asked about getting his belongings, just as he has not asked where I am moving to.

I pile his old camping gear and some boxes of papers he has carted around toward the front of the garage. There is an extensive collection of tools and a box of miscellaneous plugs and extension cords to go through.

"I don't need any of this." He waves his arm, encompassing the entire garage.

"You don't want anything?" I am surprised. "What about the

drill? Or this ax that was your grandfather's?"

"No." He stands on the threshold, looking in.

"Okay. Well, I guess it's on to the books."

He reaches into the pile of tools and pulls out a hammer with a wooden handle. "I'll take this."

Later, I will laugh as I tell this story. He walked out of my life with only a hammer. I think he fancied himself as a young man in love. How tedious and inconvenient it was for him to be confronted by a sixty-one-year-old wife amid the rubbish of a life.

***

One evening, as the taped-up boxes accumulate around me and I am sweaty and tired, I call it a day. I pour some wine and watch *Out of Africa*, a movie based on the memoir by Isak Dinesen. In the story, a young Danish woman (played by Meryl Streep) travels in the early 1900s to the British colony in Kenya. She marries, starts a coffee farm, and soon after, her husband leaves. She then falls in love with Denys (played by Robert Redford) and Kenya, but ends up losing him and her farm and is forced to leave Kenya. When I first saw the movie almost thirty years ago, I left the theater and read everything by Isak Dinesen I could find. She was an incredible writer and storyteller. At the time, I resolved to never turn away from adventure and to be as strong as she was after losing everything.

There is a scene near the end of the movie when she is sitting among boxes as she prepares to go back to Denmark. Denys comes to say goodbye. She tells him of this game she's been playing with herself, thinking of how good it all was. When she can't bear it one more second, she forces herself to think of one more thing. And then she knows she can bear anything. She invites Denys to help her by dancing with her one last time. A waltz plays on her Victrola, and they dance among the boxes and out to the moonlit lawn.

I look up from my own boxes and call Perry. I invite him out to dinner tomorrow to mark our wedding anniversary. My version of our last dance. Enough wine makes this a good idea. He agrees to dinner.

As I get ready the next evening, I imagine us having a teary moment. Not reuniting, exactly. Some part of me knows we're past that place; my imagination won't let me get that far. But as I imagine us at Café Med, our favorite restaurant, I picture Perry, under the influence of alcohol, finally opening up. I imagine a dim sense of understanding emerging, one that will bring pain but also closure. I select my outfit carefully, a dress Perry always liked, and I wear the blue topaz pendant he gave me. I picture us at our usual table.

An hour before we are due to meet, Perry cancels.

CHAPTER 26

The day before the movers come, Perry and I finally finish dividing the last of our books. When we're done, he tells me he's put beer in the fridge and asks if I want one. The day is hot, and the bees flit among the flowers in the gardens.

"Sure." I shrug.

We sit out on the deck together one last time. He tells me he's been staying with his niece and her boyfriend, who, it turns out, have a large marijuana-growing enterprise in their basement. His niece called earlier to say they'd gotten raided and Perry shouldn't come back to the house. The boyfriend's been arrested. Now Perry's anxious he'll also be arrested.

I start laughing. "Our life sure has taken a bizarre turn."

He seems astounded at first that I'm making light of this drama, but soon joins in laughing. "Yeah." He shakes his head as if in disbelief.

We watch the chipmunks scamper around the immense rock. "I like your new glasses," he says.

"Thank you."

Suddenly, he's sobbing and can't breathe.

"Words. Give me words," I demand.

After a while, he gets out, "I am so sad about leaving this beautiful house and place."

I go cold. He doesn't say he's sad about leaving me.

He gives me a long look. "Ann has left graduate school and gone home to Vietnam. I've decided to put in for retirement and move to Vietnam to be with her."

Fuck you, I think, and I am startled by this anger. *I* don't get to retire.

I stand up. "Then you'd better get a move on filling out your paperwork that the lawyer needs for this divorce you want. I need to get back to packing."

After Perry left me, I did a lot of crying, but mostly not with him. I no longer feel safe crying with him. I cry on my own time. His weeping around me is only a screen for him to hide behind.

I know I can live alone. Some people hate eating out unaccompanied or going to the movies by themselves or taking solitary walks or traveling solo. I don't have those particular concerns.

But how do you stop loving? If he had died, no one would expect me to stop loving.

Many people who love me think Perry is a complete asshole. How do you grieve an asshole? Can I still love an asshole? No one understands this. Despite the outpouring of love and support from family and friends, I feel very alone.

***

The scheduling of the move is not ideal. The movers come on a Friday, and I have to be in Durham for the final signing over of the house the following Monday. I can't move into the Boston house until September, so during August, I will be in limbo, couch surfing with my sons' families. I decide to splurge and find a bed and breakfast in Portsmouth for the weekend. I need rest.

The day the movers come, it pours. I have an overblown notion the house and the gardens are tearfully saying goodbye to me. But the movers can't get their truck up the steep drive. All those carefully packed and taped cartons of books, clothes, and photographs get soaked as the movers trudge up and down the hill, loading the truck.

After they drive away, I pack my car with what I'll need for the next month and begin cleaning the house for the new owners. The empty rooms echo. I feel hollowed out.

Perry offered to come and help with this last phase of the moving process, but I don't want him here witnessing my misery and looking awkward as he tries to hide his relief that it is finally over.

When I get to the Inn at Strawbery Banke, I am dirty, sweaty, hungry, and numb. Sally, the owner, in her late fifties with short blond hair and a yoga body, greets me with the usual questions. Where was I traveling from? Did I need any recommendations for what to see or where to eat during my stay?

I blurt out my whole sad story. I feel unhinged, confiding in a stranger like this, but she tells me her divorce prompted her to buy this place and raise her daughters here. She lives in the back. I think she is telling me there are still good surprises to come. And maybe that's true.

I used to have inklings, whiffs of thought that carried me forth into new possibilities. But my imagination has dulled. All I can conceive of is trudging through meaningless tasks until I die. I can't picture getting excited by new passions or planning new adventures at this age.

I bump my suitcase up the narrow, steep stairs to my room and plop myself on the canopied bed. I'm worn out.

The inn is two hundred years old and two blocks from the harbor and Prescott Park. Over the years, I have often taken my walks in Prescott Park and have favorite benches where I read and write while watching the gulls fish in the water. I tell Sally that although I am moving to Boston, I will still be traveling to Maine once a week until I can transfer my job, and I will need a place to stop over on the way back, especially if the weather is awful.

Over the next year, I will leave Boston at 5 a.m., drive to Maine for work, and return to Sally's at the end of the day. This allows me to attend my New Hampshire writers' group and see friends. Sally usually closes the inn during the cold, quiet months, but this winter, as a favor, she makes up one room for me and leaves the key under a brick by the front door. She wakes early to brew a pot of coffee for me by 6:30. During that time, even people who don't know me nurture me well. It helps enormously.

Now, I make a special point to be more conscious of random humans around me. I pass out compliments to store clerks, ask how they're doing, give money to anyone who asks on the street, and smile when I catch someone's eye as we're passing on the sidewalk. Tiny gestures, I know, but ones that remind me that, for that moment, I am not alone.

CHAPTER 27

One month after leaving my New Hampshire life, four months after Perry left, I join the tens of thousands who, on September first, clog the narrow streets of Boston with moving trucks. Most are students at one of the twenty-five-plus colleges and universities in the metro Boston area. Everyone appears excited. Starting. Starting college, starting a first job, moving to a first apartment off campus, or starting a new life together as a couple.

Most have U-Hauls with the orange logo and the truck with the back ramp that takes up two parking spaces. I stand on the porch of my new house and watch the scene. Clumps of young people carry boxes and march up and down the metal ramps so that they clang on the asphalt. A few houses down, I hear a group of students laughing and teasing each other about being weaklings and challenging one another to a contest of how many boxes one person can carry up three flights of stairs. Occasionally, there's a shout—*Watch that corner! Lift, lift!*—as a couch or a desk is maneuvered through a narrow doorframe.

My moving truck, with professional movers, is due in a few hours. Louise, my brother John's widow, is scrubbing the kitchen and I go back inside to join her. Two gray-haired ladies scouring floors doesn't fit with the boisterous sounds of the young people moving in down the street. Louise is seventy-one and never stops talking. Her chatter strains my nerves, but she's come all the way from Florida to help me. I am beyond grateful.

The apartment upstairs, where Shirley lived her entire life, is immaculate. Before she left, she washed and starched all the curtains. Because it is the larger apartment, that is where my tenants will live.

Zac has spent these past weeks interviewing prospective renters. He settled on a group of friends who wanted to start a co-op. He arranged to install a new bathroom and build a sixth bedroom. What he accomplished for me is astounding. I have become a landlady, a new, totally unfamiliar role. I imagine myself dispensing wisdom and solace as needed. The six people who will live upstairs have begun their working lives doing good works, spending their time in various progressive nonprofits.

My apartment has the accumulated grime from 124 years of renters. It's hot, sweaty work. I love it. The task is clear and the result gratifying. Finally, I have caught a bit of the excitement in the air as it wafts through the city. A start. A new beginning. My muscles are strong as I lug pails of water and mop the grimy floor for the second time. I'm almost cheerful.

***

The last time I felt the rush of a brand-new beginning from a move was when I left my childhood home on Long Island in 1970. It was the winter of my senior year of high school. That autumn, I'd read Aldous Huxley's *The Doors of Perception*, Robert Heinlein's *Stranger in a Strange Land*, and Hermann Hesse's *Siddhartha*. It was the dawning of the Age of Aquarius. The body was not shameful; it was beautiful. Sex was not dirty and secretive; it was loving and giving.

Dan, who was in college in Buffalo by then, had come home for a weekend visit. He was trying to convince me we should start a commune together. Communes at that time were popping up across the country, groups of people buying land in rural areas, farming and living together. His plan was to gather some of our friends to live cheaply in Buffalo, and to work and save money to buy property.

That day, we'd gone to Jones Beach to walk. The wind pulled his long hair from the rubber band that held it back. It streamed behind him, occasionally whipping across his face. He brushed it away impatiently.

"People have gotten too disconnected from the land," he said. "They eat processed food and live in little boxes on the hillside. Do you want to live like your parents? Scared of change, talking about which restaurant they went to last week?"

We hiked through the sand. The day was brilliant, the sun reflecting off the water. Only the very top layer of sand was warm to the touch. October beach. Clear, windy, empty. Great swells built in the distance, rolled toward shore, shrank, flattened out, and gently lapped the sand. "I'm not sure dropping out from the world is the way," I said.

"We'll be with people who say what they feel, who respect each other totally, who won't abuse the world's resources—"

I interrupted him. "A lot of good that will do when the bomb drops. It will drop on your perfect little commune in the same way it will drop on the shopping malls." When Dan got going, there was nothing to do but interrupt. He spoke without breathing.

"Wild," my father had called him years ago, soon after we'd met. Then he added, "Be careful. This one cares only about himself."

My mother had shaken her head. "Look who's calling the kettle black!"

At the time, I'd thought it ridiculous. Dan was nothing like my father, and he was anything but selfish. He had dreams. He had ideals. He was a radical.

On the beach that day, Dan walked as fast as he talked. His long legs covered a lot of ground. I had to run a little to catch up.

"People have to learn to relate," he said. "Look at all these people who are fucked up in their personal lives."

"But—" I started.

"The institutions are not going to change," he talked over me.

"Well—" I tried again.

"No bullshit. Honesty. We'll make a world where people are honest with each other."

"Dan!" I remember yelling to get his attention. Sometimes his style of conversation was like a battering ram.

"The institutions are fucked," he kept going. "Why should we be fucked up with them?"

Even at the time, I thought his arguments lacked depth. But I felt as wide and open as the ocean. The world was changing. Anything was possible. Plus, things at home had gotten difficult. Ken's wife, June, had left him, and he'd moved back home with his two little boys. My mother had learned of my father's affair and was drinking heavily.

"Come with me," Dan said that day, putting his arms out and taking my hands. "I need you."

Three little words.

Magic words.

I explained it all to my mother. "Isn't it weird that in all these houses, each one has a washing machine? Why not one machine for five or ten houses? We don't all need to have our own."

"You try sharing a washing machine with Mrs. Malloy and her ten kids," my mother said, distracted and not believing I would do something so foolish.

I was eager to be off and start changing the world. So much needed to be done, and I saw no reason to stick around and finish high school. I wanted to ride wild elephants and travel over mountains. I wanted to talk to people you're not supposed to talk to on the city streets. I wanted to say yes, yes, yes instead of maybe, or I don't know, or I'm not sure if I should. I wanted to live far away in a village in India or Africa and understand what life is like. I wanted to climb way out on the jetty and dance right there on those slippery rocks with the water all around, not be afraid of falling, and let the force of the sea seep through me, be like the ocean and travel the world.

It was very cold that January morning, the day I left home. Way below freezing. The ground was hard, the dirt frozen into little ruts, the grass brown. The sky was gray, that sharp metal gray of early winter mornings. My mother was in her flannel bathrobe, and my father was dressed in his suit for work.

I turned to hug my mother goodbye. My friends Mitch and Judy would be there any minute, and together, we'd drive to Buffalo and start a whole different life. My mother started to cry, which started me crying.

"Let's not have a scene," my father said. He got up from the table where he'd been drinking his coffee and walked out. He returned carrying a tan furry thing slung over his arm. "I got you this. A going-away present. Wholesale. It's rabbit. You will never be cold in this. Try it on." He held it up for me.

I wrapped myself in the coat, petted its fur, and exclaimed about how beautiful it was, how soft, how warm, how wonderful. I hugged my father and felt him kiss the top of my head. But I knew I would never wear the coat. No way I could walk around wearing dead animals on my back.

My father reached for my woolen pea coat.

"No, I'll take that too." I held onto it firmly. "I'll wear it when I'm changing tires or something. I wouldn't want to ruin this."

"Do you think being able to change your own tires brings you independence from a man?" my mother asked. "That's it? It doesn't matter that you are only seventeen and running off to live with him, as long as you change your own tires? That means you are a modern woman?"

"This coat is so warm, I'm sweating." I shrugged it off. Where the fuck were Mitch and Judy? A new world was starting out there, a new way of living, and I was going to be part of it whether my mother approved or not. We'd been having the same conversations for weeks now. "It's not like we're getting married," I added.

"That's supposed to make me feel better?" She sat down and picked up her coffee cup. "There are reasons why women get married. But no, you give it all away for free."

"What?"

"You love Dan; he loves you. So, off you go together. This is not a new story. But has he said, let's get married, I'll care for you, I'll work hard for you, I'll stick around? No. He says, come live in Buffalo with seven other people in the middle of January with the snow piling up."

"We don't believe in relationships like that. We don't believe in the man working hard to protect and support the woman. We believe in equality, in each person pulling equal weight, in everyone having an equal voice, in—"

My mother cut me off. "Great. You'll get to cook and clean and change tires, and he'll talk about how wonderful he is because he believes in equality." Her fingers drummed on the table. "Make sure you always keep a little money aside, separate, for you."

"That won't be necessary." I waved in dismissal. "We have a completely honest relationship. That's the whole point. Open. No hiding anything, no parts of ourselves."

"God help you."

***

Forty-four years later, I am again at a beginning. At sixty-one.

I've experienced adventures and drama, but nothing that I'd envisioned on that icy winter day.

With lots of help from friends and family, Louise and I got the house set up in a few days. I'm not one to live with unpacked boxes cluttering my home for long. Extra dressers, end tables, bookshelves, boxes and boxes of papers, boxes of photographs, the assorted tools, and more all go down to the basement. I suggest to the tenants upstairs that they go furniture "shopping" on my side of the basement and take whatever they can use.

In my apartment, nothing fits right. I put the small section of the couch under the front windows and flank it with all the Christmas cacti Shirley left for me. She was excited not to have to worry about any maintenance ever again, including watering houseplants.

She also found me a picture of her grandparents and their five children taken in the late 1800s. In the photograph, they sit, arranged formally in the tiny yard behind my house, against the wrought iron fence that still borders Forest Hills Cemetery. The cemetery was founded in 1848. As a secular burial place, a garden, an arboretum, and a sculpture garden, it was designed to offer people a way to connect with nature.

Now, on the other side of the fence, a large border of woods exists before the formal grounds begin. Shirley told me that when she was a girl, it was a field with blueberry bushes. I decide to frame the photo and hang it in the entranceway.

I arrange the larger couch section along one wall and my bookshelves along the other. The wood floors are dark and in terrible shape, but the rugs Perry and I bought together cover most of the bad spots. My desk and more bookshelves go in the study, along with a futon for guests. The study window overlooks the woods. Perry and I bought an old second-hand dining table with several leaves that can accommodate fourteen people for dinner, but it shrinks to nothing. This goes into the dining room, which will also double as a play space for my grandkids. The basket that used to hold the wood for our stove is now full of toys from Ricky that her granddaughter has outgrown. My bedroom is in the back, and our king-size bed takes up the space and becomes a great jumping place for my grandchildren. An antique kitchen hutch that was my brother John's is in the kitchen.

Within two days, I have a home.

The kids and grandkids come over for dinner. We christen my new place with a takeout Indian feast. Everyone oohs and ahhs about how beautiful it looks already.

After they leave, I wander the house, trying to make sense of the fact that I now live here.

Alone.

What I miss most is the touching. Not the sex, although I miss that too. Perry was a creative lover. Early in our relationship, when we made love multiple times a day, I told my women's group that I felt like a dusty houseplant that had been rescued from the dark den and set out on a bright windowsill, watered, fed, and misted. My leaves were perky, my stem sturdy and flexible. They had groaned at the over-the-topness.

But it's the touching I miss most. The spontaneous hugs. The kissing as we woke up, left for the day, returned in the evening, passed in the hallway, and said good night. My head in his lap as we binge-watched our shows and he played with my hair. The foot rubs when he sat on the other end of the couch while I was reading and pulled my feet into his hands. Holding hands as we walked. Holding hands sometimes, even as we sat next to each other doing nothing. Tick checks at the end of a long walk. His hand on the small of my back. Holding his face, rubbing his temples, massaging his shoulders, kissing his jawbone. Spooning, being enveloped in his arms.

***

In the morning, I wake up thinking about the birds at the Durham house. I had a dream that a red-crested pileated woodpecker was sitting on a branch outside our bedroom window, and I had called for Perry to come see.

It wasn't possible; there were no branches that close to the bedroom window. But I could sit outside, very still, and the birds, butterflies, dragonflies would land close by. And inside, from my study in the loft, I watched as black-capped chickadees, finches, and cardinals called to each other in the trees.

I had never bird-watched before meeting Perry.

It was a great excuse for us to go tramping around in the woods or marshes. We often went to the Rachel Carson Nature Preserve or to Laudholm Farm in Maine. Of course, we could also just sit in our house with its six sides of windows, high up on the hill and no one around.

We took such pleasure in these things, carrying our binoculars and bird books, watching the foxes, the deer run behind our house, and the woodpeckers all around. It was never quiet. The sound of birds and wildlife was loud enough for people to comment when I was on the phone with them. The woodpeckers hammered, the squirrels screeched and scampered through the woods, the foxes chirped and howled.

And those were merely the usual visitors. After two seasons of gardening and losing vegetables and flowers to the hedgehogs, the deer, the possums, and the slugs, I remembered I was the visitor and let it go, grateful to have such a close view.

When I thought about it later, I realized Perry and I had developed a world of living in the present. *What would you like to eat?*

Where should we walk today? How about sketching on the Marginal Way? It wasn't planned exactly, but when I came home with talk of frustration with my bosses, rants about the criminal justice system, or worries about my kids, he would listen for a bit and then suggest we watch a movie and let it all go.

I am a processor. I like to gnaw at an issue until I've sucked all the marrow from the bone and there is no meat left. *What did that facial expression mean? Do you think your sister really meant it when she said she was doing okay?* Sometimes, this intense focus made Perry anxious. Gradually, I edited myself. It didn't matter, I thought. I had plenty of other people with whom I could grind those concerns to dust.

Perry is a bone burrower. His style is to sink those worries deep, plant a flower on top, and hope the worries vanish. Since we both were aware of his hesitancy to launch into sharing distressing confidences, we developed a shorthand that we called taking our emotional temperatures. It was a signal that went both ways, a sign for each of us that meant we were not distracted, but were open and wanting to listen if the other one wanted to talk about potentially difficult feelings.

Until he left, I hadn't realized how much our discourse had become the birds out the window, the foxes in the meadow, the snow on the drive. Or the books we were reading or newspaper articles to share. It had happened gently over time. For me, it felt so connected, this living in the present tense with another human. So comforting.

But obviously, what he chose not to talk about was considerable.

***

After a great rupture, all that you know to be true about your life, the way you breathe, the way your feet land on the earth, the way you shop for groceries, is gone and has to be relearned all over again.

The woman who married Perry and me was a friend from childhood with whom I'd discovered box turtles and read in the trees. She moved away in the sixth grade, and we lost contact, but when Perry and I decided to marry, we searched for a Unitarian minister and I found her again.

I learn that the month Perry left me, she had a stroke. A great rupture. She literally had to learn to walk and talk and move on the earth all again.

My rupture seems so minor next to hers. Yet for me, inside, I am having a difficult time remembering to breathe. Remembering how.

***

I remind myself I will be fine. I am not lonely for people with whom to discuss world events, work events, or the intimate, emotional details of life. I am not lonely for people to share my walks. Roz asked me to go to Costa Rica with her. Susan and I will attend conferences. Linda said yes to a trip to Scotland. Diane will take me clothes shopping and to book readings. Ricky will take me makeup shopping and to writing classes. Bett, Margaret, Julie, Paula, Titia, and Martha will have drinks with me. Cyrisse will go with me to the movies. Greg will take me out to dinner and to plays. I can explore Boston with my grandchildren. I can eat with my children and cook for them.

It is enough. It is more than enough, actually. It is rather wonderful.

***

During my first week in the new house, Perry calls. We still have a lot of paperwork to do to complete the filing for divorce, but we've spoken little. I sit on the couch that once was in front of our woodstove. "Maybe I fucked up," he says. "Maybe I shouldn't have left."

"What are you saying?"

"I miss you. Everywhere I go, I see something that reminds me of you and me together."

"Me too," I say. Even though I've moved to Boston, far away from our Durham home, there are reminders of him everywhere: the walks we took along the Charles River or through the Fenway into the Public Gardens. On my drive north to work in Maine, I pass the coastal routes we took. In Portsmouth, when I stay over at Sally's, I walk the brick sidewalks and pass Café Med where we used to share mussels, the art supply store where we bought water-color paints, and the library where we spent hours.

Sometimes, when I stay at Sally's, I pour wine into my travel mug and take my cigarettes to a bench by the harbor in Prescott Park and watch the lobster boats, tugboats, and barges. I write long emails to Perry, describing the view and reminding him of the plan we had to live in Portsmouth for a few years after we sold the Durham house and before moving to Boston. I don't send them. I've yet to formulate the perfect email that will both stab him in the heart and not sound pathetic or deranged. That he still refuses to talk about what led to his decision to leave continues to make me nuts.

But perhaps it's better this way. It's possible he's saved us years of sulks and tears and stony silences. But I know this isn't true. It simply saved him from having to participate in those tearful sessions.

Sometimes I write in my journal about how, as I walk the streets and explore the cemetery near Strawbery Banke, I'm trying to reclaim Portsmouth for myself. I don't want this city to be all about Perry and our life together. I walk the streets with my head up and shoulders back; people smile at me, and I smile back. I want to create a new image of aging that accepts the realities—but doesn't devolve into aging being only about pain and loss from the unplanned changes in my body and my circumstances.

***

I want this heartache to go away. But do I want Perry back? If we were together now, I would examine every eyebrow move, every mouth muscle, every touch for what he wasn't expressing in words, for what he wasn't telling me. I would never be able to trust his present-tense way of being again.

The morning after Perry's call, as I sit outside on the back porch, I start a new journal. *The Perry Leaving Journal* was all about him and what prompted him to leave. This journal will be all about me and what I want. I remember in my twenties when the kids were little and I was married to Dan, that one day I practiced in front of a mirror saying the words *I want, I am, I need,* so they would slide more easily out of my mouth.

Sitting on my porch overlooking the woods, hearing the birds in the trees, I tell myself that I don't have to decide anything about Perry at this moment. After all, he actually didn't say he wanted to come back. We'd been here before.

I title my new journal, *Learning to Live Without Perry*. But I cross that out and write *Gin Flourishes*. Every hour on the hour, the bells from the cemetery chime. I see my first hummingbird on the rose of Sharon, a bush that Shirley's mother planted. The drama and shock of Perry leaving is intense. But I know drama and shock always fade.

CHAPTER 28

During the week, as much as I can between work obligations, I arrange to hang out with my grandchildren. This serves many purposes. It helps their parents, gets me outside and out of my own head, and I'm bathed in love.

I have a delightful morning walking Didi's baby doll, Lola, an anatomically correct male doll, up and down the hill and into the community garden, where we collect rocks and marigolds.

Afterward, instead of hanging pictures or organizing my clothes or dealing with paperwork, I lie down. It's been a wild four months. I decide that having a rest day is permitted. My phone dings with a text from Perry about a field trip with his students to Barnes & Noble. I stare at it. It's such an intimate message in a certain way, part of the minutiae of life that we used to pass back and forth. It is also presumptuous on his part to send it, to count on me to care.

I want to call a friend to discuss this, but at this point, the people who love and support me and keep me upright are tired of the Perry saga. They don't miss Perry. Their responses have changed.

They no longer go on about how Perry is a fool, a jerk, an asshole. Now, the judgments feel directed at me. Some are gentle. "Is it good for you to keep taking his texts and emails?" a friend might ask. Others are more direct. "You can never get back with him!" Some friends issue directives: "Block his texts and emails!" Some are weary, and their responses are short: "Ugh! OMG." But the message from everyone is the same. *Don't keep engaging. Cut him off. Move on.*

What I want everyone to tell me is that I have been amazing. I want them to notice that I have accomplished so much: I have sold my house, changed my work location, changed my life. I want gold stars. I want them to say how I'm flourishing, like the title of my new journal. I want the words to be true.

CHAPTER 29

I join Sing Positive, a multigenerational community chorus in which both my sons and their families participate. It's unsettling. It feels like I have entered into someone else's life and live in someone else's apartment. Much is familiar—the furniture, the rugs, the pictures—yet all is different.

But then, after I arrive home from a long workday, the doorbell rings. "Hey, Nons," comes a voice through the mail slot in the door. "It's Dar." This is my three-year-old grandson, who's been permitted to cross the street alone and ring the bell.

I laugh. Living in Jamaica Plain is excellent.

Perry keeps calling, in addition to emailing and texting, to talk about how complicated his life has become. He tells me his feelings of missing me are growing stronger, not weaker. I'm not sure how to even think about this. For me, I refuse to miss him; or at least, I'm working on making that true. I am angry at myself whenever I miss him. Another part is pleased when he misses me, just like Otis Redding croons: "You don't miss your water 'til your well run dry."

***

In my journal, I start a list of all the things I don't miss about Perry. I don't miss how apprehensive he'd become before attending a large family gathering. I don't miss how he'd buy broccoli when we already had two bunches yellowing in the fridge. I don't miss the last-minute change of plans or his *let's play it by ear* way of organizing life.

I am in Maine, and in between seeing clients, when I get an

email from Perry. He has ended things with Ann. As far as I knew, after our divorce becomes final, after he finishes the school year, he was planning to retire and go live with her in Vietnam.

I call Ricky on the drive home, wondering what to make of this information. Perry's become a windstorm with such onslaughts of emotional crosswinds, I no longer can think. I'm hoping she can at least tell me what I feel.

She can't.

But she does tell me what *she* feels. "He's a fucking dickhead who's being sadistic. Why is he telling you this shit?"

My mom once counseled me about the dangers of "giving it away for free" with Dan, and now I wonder if I'm doing the same with Perry. Except instead of sex, I'm supplying emotional support. Perry wants to lean on me and rely on me, and he assumes I will pick up the phone and listen. Part of me wants to turn him away, and part of me is obsessively curious about what is going on.

Perry calls soon after I hang up with Ricky. The call is under the pretext of a question about filling out yet another divorce form. He tells me he ended things with Ann because of a lack of trust. "Maybe she just wanted a green card after all," he says.

He starts babbling about the plane ticket he bought and how to get a refund. He wonders if he can stop the process of retiring from the school district. He's got no money, hates his apartment because he has nothing to come home to, and needs to get back to playing tennis. It's a word deluge. When he winds down, I ask again if he's thought about going into therapy and getting some help. "You don't sound well," I remark.

"That's as it should be because I'm not well." He pauses and then says, "I often think of being able to be with you again and finding peace, happiness, and health."

He makes being with me sound like a brochure for a deluxe

spa or a sanitarium.

I repeat that he needs to get himself into therapy. "You've ended two relationships in four months," I point out.

After I end the call, I feel shaken. Even though Perry left, we are still technically married. If he's got dementia, if he's in psychological or emotional trouble, I believe I still have a responsibility. Or then again, maybe I don't. Marriage vows need to be more specific. *In sickness and in health* isn't clear enough if it's the sickness that causes the marriage to end.

I am bungee jumping through emotions. One moment, I'm bereaved and aching. Another moment, I am telling him we must continue with the divorce. And then I'm back to sighing and sniffling and listening to "Another Somebody Done Somebody Wrong Song" on my back porch in the dark.

I know this is to be expected. Feelings are not linear; they loop and whirl and spiral. I promise to let myself feel whatever comes up and not judge anything as right or wrong, good or bad.

But all this "feeling" is exhausting, and I decide it's okay to distract myself. I hang a few pictures, put away some papers, do a quick food shop, and visit with Zac and Cynthia. We have a long talk about how to deal with their baby's sleep issues. I get the heat working and the old, warped windows closed. We're having a late-September cold spell.

I am invited to go to a sixtieth birthday party for Lisa from the community garden. I decline. I can't deal with being social with new people. I'm invited to my ex-husband Dan's house to see two old friends in from California who we went to high school with. I don't want to do that either. I feel too vulnerable. I say no.

That's okay, I tell myself. I am doing the very best I can.

***

During the first few years of my life, my father worked rotating shifts in the fire department. If he came home before my bedtime, I would run down the hall, sprint past my brothers' room where they were doing homework, and leap off the stairs into his waiting arms. He stood on the landing with a huge grin on his face. I had absolute trust.

I was a daddy's girl.

"She has that man wrapped around her little finger," I heard my mother tell her friends. I didn't know exactly what that meant, but I knew my mother didn't think it was good.

When my father was home, I followed him around as he worked in the yard or fixed things in the house. He had a room in the basement called *the dungeon* where he kept paint and tools. He had an enclosed space on the side of the garage called *the shed*, where all the lawn and gardening tools were kept. He would give me jobs. "Pick up all the fallen apples so we can mow the lawn." I felt proud and helpful even though the apples were rotten, and my fingers sank into the squishy parts. As we worked side by side, we'd talk about whatever I was learning in school or what I was reading.

"How did you get to be so wise?" he'd often say. I don't remember what that was ever in response to. I simply remember feeling special when he said it.

My mother would call, "Ginny, it's time to come in and set the table."

My father would answer, "Let her be, Edie."

I felt my parents' competition for my affection, but there was no contest. I was my father's. Father was the light, my mother the dark. His face lit up when I walked into a room. *How's my bright-eyed girl? Look at that ski-jump nose. You're brown as a berry.*

On weekend afternoons, my father would occasionally lie on the living room floor next to the stereo and close his eyes as he listened to opera. If he caught me walking by, he would exclaim,

"Listen. Listen. Hear that voice, those notes."

He promised to take me to the opera when I was older. But by the time I was age-appropriate, other parts of his life had taken over.

He also loved to say, "Kittens always grow up to be cats."

My father hated cats.

***

When I was fourteen, my brother John joined the Peace Corps and went away to India. My other brother, Ken, moved to New Jersey with his wife and sons. My parents bought a condo on a little strip of land on the southern coast of Long Island. My mother and I stayed there all summer, and my father came out on the weekends.

On one side of that condo was the Atlantic Ocean; on the other side was Great South Bay. I learned to sail a sunfish. It's basically a flat board with a mast, sail, and removable keel that can skim over shallow areas. Easily tipped but also easily righted.

My parents would go ocean-side and sit with friends, and I would go bay-side and take out the boat. The bay was huge. I could not see from one side to the other. On certain days, the wind would whip the water and create choppy waves. Deep channels had been dug to accommodate large boats, and there was a lot of traffic. Sailing west, I could go all the way to Fire Island. If I wasn't careful, I could end up in the Atlantic Ocean.

It was tricky getting out of the small cove and into the bay. If the wind was right and I tacked correctly, I could zoom right out. I had learned to sail but was inexperienced, and I often ran aground. Frequently, I tipped over. No life jacket, of course.

I tried to stay clear of the channel and avoid the full-sized boats, but I didn't have great control. Still, I loved the adventure. At fourteen, there was great freedom in zipping across the bay to the far shore, the wind tugging the sail, seeing all the fancy estates, skinny dipping in coves, and landing on sandbars.

When a sailboat changes direction, the boom swings fast. In a Sunfish, you duck out of the way and hop to the other side. The wind catches the sail and tips the boat so the sail skims the water. You use your body as a counterweight so you don't capsize.

If you turn one way, the boom snaps across; if you turn another, it floats across.

One cloudless day that summer, I was skimming along, breeze in my hair, using my ninety-pound body to lean against the wind, heading toward the middle of the bay, crossing the channel with the big boats.

A fog dropped. It didn't roll in from the distance but instantly dropped. A flash fog, dense and thick.

I could see nothing. I knew enough to let out the sail and slow the boat. All around, I could hear the low rumble of foghorns as the larger boats dropped anchor, warning other boats away.

I had no anchor. The fog was so complete, I had no sensation of movement. I held out my arm and could not see my hand. I wasn't particularly concerned. I imagined I was scarcely drifting.

Then *whack*. The boom swung, and I jumped out of the way, changing sides, still holding the sail loose. *Whack*. The boom swung back. I had no point of reference, nothing to clue me to movement except for the boom swinging. I realized I was turning in circles.

The fog lifted as quickly as it had fallen. All over the bay, boats were scattered where they'd dropped anchor or run aground. I had come within inches of crashing into a large cabin cruiser. I was on the far shore in a place I'd never been.

This is betrayal. No sense of direction, no up, no down, no point of reference, only that boom, *whack, whack,* allowing me to understand I was going in circles.

One Saturday, later that summer, my father took me to play tennis down the road from the beach. He would lob balls over the net, running me from one side of the court to the other, and I would send them back, the ball whizzing low over the net. As we finished, a woman came up to us, all smiles, and complimented me on my tennis skills. She said how much she enjoyed watching us and how beautiful I was with my long, tanned legs.

"I'm Ila." She held out her hand to my father.

My father shook her hand. "Joe DeLuca. And this is my daughter, Ginny."

It turned out that she and her teenage son were renting a little house farther down the beach. "He's about your age," she said to me. Soon enough, she and her son were invited for cocktails. This was not unusual. Both the vacation nature of the place and my father's sociability made this kind of interaction commonplace.

While our parents had drinks, I took Dorian for a walk down the long boardwalk. He was taller than I was, with blond hair and a cute smile, but he was very serious. He told me his older brother had died in February in a skiing accident. He had skied into a tree and died of internal injuries.

"That's so weird," I said. "My father's secretary called this winter to tell my father that her son had a serious skiing accident, crashing into a tree. Her son died too."

My mother had been furious that day. We had been eating Sunday dinner in the dining room with its velvet silver-flecked wallpaper. As my father rushed to leave for the hospital, my mother kept asking why his secretary would call my father and not her own family.

The following day on the beach, sitting on the sand and reading our books, I told my parents I was going for a walk down the beach. "Maybe that boy Dorian will be swimming."

My father, who never raised his voice and rarely said no to me, said, "No. You can't do that."

"Why not?"

"Don't be a hussy," he said.

I was stunned. His words felt like a slap in the face.

Later, Ila called. Dorian wanted to know if I would go to the movies with him.

My first date.

Ila drove us the twenty minutes into town and picked us up when the movie ended. We saw *Elvira Madigan*, a film about young lovers who run away, eat strawberries and cream, can't make it, and commit suicide together. Dorian didn't say one word the entire time. It was awkward, to say the least.

***

Years later, when I was in college and soon after my father left my mother, I learned that Ila was the woman he'd left her for. I realized that it had been Ila, not his secretary, who called that Sunday to say her son had been in a terrible skiing accident. I remember being incredulous. They forced Dorian to pretend not to know my father while setting me up on a date with him? I wondered in what universe they decided that was a good idea. But I don't remember feeling much more than that. It was something I talked about with close friends, a can-you-believe-this story. So creepy.

I would also learn that the affair with Ila had been going on since I was nine. Every Tuesday and Thursday, when my father ostensibly went on business trips to Boston, he was actually with Ila and Dorian in New York.

My father had another family.

When I saw Dorian some years after my father died, he referred to my father as "Dad."

Betrayals happen in many forms.

When you are betrayed, it's more than anger, disbelief, or sadness that someone you trusted and loved could be cruel. Eventually, you do have all those responses, but initially, it's bewilderment. It's the flash fog, when all reference points disappear and you're stuck in place, going in circles.

CHAPTER 30

In early October, the lawyer's assistant calls to tell me Perry and I didn't file some initial form the court needed so it could process all the other paperwork. "Why didn't you do that?" she asks.

I get testy. "I'm kind of relying on you all," I reply.

I wonder if they ask Perry the same question. Why am I getting put on the spot?

So, on my way back from Maine, I call and arrange with Perry to meet in Portsmouth to sign the form. I need this divorce to be finalized. I am exhausted by it all.

I meet Perry at Rudi's, a hamburger place on Congress Street. He hasn't shaved, his shirt is wrinkled. We sign the form while waiting for our food.

"You look wonderful," he tells me.

I'm dressed for work, wearing a new bright red jacket. My curly hair, which changes with the weather, is in perfect form today.

"I know I'm a mess. I'm too depressed to do laundry," he says, and laughs a little.

I again ask him about finding a therapist.

He nods. "Probably a good idea."

He tells me he saw old colleagues of his who'd moved away, and how upset they were to hear of our breakup.

"Did you tell them why we broke up?"

"No."

"Have you told anyone from work why?"

He shakes his head no.

"Well, just so you know, I've told quite a few people," I say cheerfully. "I've told them that my husband left me at sixty to have babies."

He grimaces but doesn't say anything. The waitress brings our hamburgers. I fantasize about telling her too.

He mentions not having the information about the car insurance yet. I let him know his life insurance is still being billed to me. He tells me he has piles of unopened mail.

He is so adrift. I want to take care of him. The urge is powerful, but I suppress it. This is not a healthy part of me.

We move on to chitchat. I ask about his sister. He asks about the grandkids. He starts to tear up and excuses himself to go to the bathroom. When he returns, he doesn't sit back down.

"I'm losing it," he says. "Let's get the check." It doesn't seem to occur to him that I am not done eating or might want coffee. "I need to get out of here."

Making a fast exit has become his way to manage his discomfort, to avoid whatever he is feeling. I, of course, want to know *exactly what feelings* he is avoiding. But I also recognize that his refusal to answer will only enrage and frustrate me. I am left to imagine.

***

I'm straddling different worlds. It is an acrobatic feat that grows increasingly uncomfortable as my worlds slip further apart. It also involves a great deal of driving. There's my world with Perry that my heart won't let go of. My world of work in Maine. My world of friends in New Hampshire. My world in Boston that I can't quite connect with yet.

I feel shame on so many levels.

"I'm a bad husband picker." This is the line I use when asked by acquaintances about my divorce, as if I lack the skill to choose a good, ripe cantaloupe from the market.

What I am really saying, and I'm sure I fool no one, is: *It's not me! Not my fault! It's not because I'm bad in relationships. It's not because I'm unlovable.*

I want to be seen as strong, brave, and full of good humor in the face of adversity.

With every muscle fiber, with every blood vessel, I want to hold onto the woman I became with Perry—the playful, sexy, smart, funny, joyful, caring, relaxed woman. I'm afraid I'll miss her even more than I'll miss him. I want to keep that woman, even if I don't have Perry to love, our house to live in, or our city to roam.

I sincerely like that version of myself.

I am sixty-one, but it's not as if all my other ages have disappeared. No, I have expanded to include them. The little girl, proud of the fancy red bow in her hair, lives with the anxious fifth grader practicing for the spelling test and the sulky, frizzy-haired teen. Right now, I'm the toddler resisting change, my back arched, head back, mouth open, and legs like spaghetti as I'm overpowered by an adult wanting to hurry me into the car seat.

I need to figure out how all these different versions of me can coexist—and to prove to myself that the woman I was with Perry is still me.

CHAPTER 31

I need to bring my car into the shop to be fixed, and the repair shop has a car service that will drive you home and pick you up. See? Look at me, such an independent single woman. I am determined not to depend on my kids for this kind of thing. The driver is very chatty. I learn he is from Romania and has grown children doing well in college. I speak about my grandchildren. He asks where my husband is. I squirm. I don't want to say I've been left.

"I lost my husband in Vietnam," I tell him, and give him a sorrowful look. Well, it is kind of true.

I don't know who I am afraid of being judged by. When asked for demographic information, I check single instead of divorced. Why does the form care if I got dumped? How does that info help anyone? Divorce is a shame inducer coming from some early cultural imprint. Divorce equals *couldn't cut it*. Divorce equals *refusing to stay in the game*. Divorce equals *failure*.

But single is no better. Single means no one wants me. Single means lonely. Or it could mean selfishness. Single means has never been asked. Rejected.

I want a box that says courageous. Resilient. Self-sufficient, involved in community, accomplished.

***

One week after meeting Perry to sign that form, I receive a copy of the divorce agreement. This paper must be notarized before it can be submitted to the court. Divorce paperwork always requires one more thing. I call Perry.

"I'm not sure we should do this," he says. "I'm not sure I want to get divorced."

"What's up with Ann?" I ask, my tone clipped.

"We're not together, but we're still in touch."

Up, down, back, forth, round and round. "Let's get the divorce," I say. "Afterwards, you can figure out what you want. I'll meet you at Citizens Bank at ten a.m. tomorrow."

The next day, at six in the morning, I get a text saying he wants to meet next week, he hasn't had a chance to review the papers.

I tell him I'm not available next week.

He shows up at the bank. He reads and weeps through the signing with the notary. As we walk to our cars, he stops midway. "I love you," he says.

I close my eyes and breathe through pain.

After we part, I buy a new computer. I am determined to invest in the writer part of me. It is, I think, the least I can do for myself.

***

That night, I dream of my brother Ken dying. It is not at all like his actual death. In my dream, I am leading a class when a staff member walks in and tells me he's been found dead. I collapse.

Like many in my family, Ken struggled with alcohol and depression. Or rather, Ken struggled with depression, and alcohol was his treatment of choice. He came of age in the 1950s. When I look back, I realize the amount of alcohol consumed by the people around me at that time was extraordinary.

And it was normalized. There were always cocktails before dinner. When my father became a salesman in New York City, he spoke of three-martini lunches. When Ken got into car accidents because he was intoxicated, it was dismissed and minimized. *He just had a few too many*. Once, when John got drunk in college, he was picked up for using the convertibles parked on the street as trampolines. This was explained as "the hijinks of youth." On weekends, neighbors would be invited over for drinks. This was "socializing."

Alcoholics were bums. Alcoholics were people like my grandmother who drank till she passed out on the weekends. Alcoholics were people who got out of control, smashed up their homes, and terrified their families. What my family did was "social drinking."

Ken worked as a store manager for Sears and Roebuck and lived in New Jersey when his sons were growing up. When he was over forty, he left that job and bought a general store in Vermont. The store sat on land that backed up to the White River and included an old farmhouse and barn. It also included, around the back, The Silver Tooth Pub.

The pub was the local drinking spot in Rochester. Ken came to know most of the town there. It was casual and clean and had a pool table. My kids loved visiting when they were little. Before the bar opened, Ken would let them play pool and pour themselves sodas. Out in front of his store, Ken grew marigolds and zinnias. He also drank copious amounts of Scotch.

After our mother died, his drinking increased. John and I convinced him to go into a treatment center, a place John found in Rhode Island. "I don't have a drinking problem," he always said. "I just like to drink. I'm never violent. I never miss work." But finally, he agreed to go.

He was there for thirty days. He tried. But after John died, Ken gave up any pretense of controlling his drinking. When I spoke to his new wife about his drinking, she said that he'd told her in no uncertain terms that if she mentioned his drinking, it was over.

Whenever I tried to talk to him about it, he got angry. Over the years, his health deteriorated.

When we got the call that my father was dying, Ken drove to

Boston so we could fly to Arizona together the following day. I woke up to see him pouring vodka into his orange juice. When did he start drinking so early in the day? I hadn't seen him in the past few months and was stunned by the change in him. He shuffled as he walked. He had a difficult time on stairs. He lost the thread of conversations. He was only fifty-seven years old.

Ken was the only member of my nuclear family who met Perry. A few years after my father died, months into my relationship with Perry, Ken was rushed to the hospital and airlifted to Dartmouth Medical Center for an aortic aneurysm. It looked like he might die. I dropped everything and drove up with his son Scott in the middle of the night. When the crisis passed and we knew he'd be fine, Perry offered to drive to Vermont and bring me back home to Boston. I thought it was the most generous gesture. Perry visited with Ken in the hospital.

Afterward, Ken told me he liked Perry a lot. "He reminds me of myself," he said, and laughed. I knew what he meant. The easy smile, the easy conversation, his steadiness and sincerity. Perry didn't make everything about himself—until he did.

Ken and his wife decided to sell the business in Vermont and move to North Carolina. Everyone thought it was a great idea, especially because Ken would be away from the bar.

Perry and I were in the throes of intense romance at the time. We'd been dating long-distance for over a year, spending every weekend together either in New Hampshire or Boston or away on an adventure.

Ken called me one day as I was preparing for Perry's arrival. I was making chocolate-covered strawberries. I'd emailed Perry earlier that week a sexy description of what use these dipped strawberries could be put to.

"My cough has gotten worse," Ken said. "The doctor suspects

lung cancer. I'm going for a biopsy."

I did not want to think of my brother dying. Ken and I talked for a long time about what would happen to his wife and his worries about his grown children if he died. I did not want to be doing this again.

Days later, I got a call from Ken's son. Ken was in the hospital, and he had lung cancer. They were going to remove the tumor. They thought it all would be fine.

I talked to Ken, and he sounded upbeat. That weekend, I went away with Perry up the coast of Maine.

Denial is powerful.

Perry and I went ocean kayaking.

When we returned, Ken's son called again.

Things were bad. Perry drove me back to New Hampshire to arrange a flight. Perry handled everything: calling the airlines, figuring out the connections, and buying the tickets. My brain was fried.

When I arrived at the hospital, Ken smiled and made jokes. He asked everyone to leave the room for a minute so he could have some time with his kid sister. When everyone left, he said, "Make this dying happen. Do this for me. Remember how you did this for John and for Mom? Do this for me too."

I nodded and left to find the nurse. I wondered how this had become my role in the family, to see everyone through. The nurse, who was deeply kind, followed me back to the room. "I hear you want some morphine," she said gently to Ken.

He asked if dying would be painful. "There will be no pain," she assured him. Soon, Ken was in a coma. He died a few hours later.

For months afterward, in private, in my journals, but never aloud, I confessed I hadn't paid enough attention. I had been in the full flower of love for Perry and had taken my eye off the ball. Of course, I know now, and probably even then, that I had no reason to feel guilt for Ken's death. It was not my fault. I had done nothing wrong. But yet, on my watch, I'd been distracted. I'd been made selfish by this new love, and Ken had died.

A week later, after I'd led a domestic violence treatment group in Dorchester, a group member was shot to death as he exited the building.

Two days later, on September eleventh, terrorist bombers flew into the World Trade Center. We were forced to delay Ken's memorial service.

Just because one bad thing happens doesn't mean others won't.

CHAPTER 32

After I have the dream about Ken dying, I vow to give up cigarettes and alcohol for thirty days. I see the dream as a missive from the dead. Smoking and drinking are disastrous ways to deal with trauma. It was perhaps understandable when I was dealing with the shock of Perry leaving, but now it is time to stop. I, of all people, should know this, given my family history.

I also vow to cut off all contact with Perry to make the transition easier. I tend to drink and smoke more when talking with him or after seeing him. Sometimes, something so obvious takes me a long time to realize.

I email Perry's sister, who hasn't been in touch since this whole leaving thing happened, and tell her that Perry seems in bad shape. Now he's *her* worry.

Perry calls that evening, and before he can tell me why, I tell him I've decided I will not respond to or initiate any calls, emails, or texts with him for the next thirty days. "I don't know what you're trying to communicate when you say you're unsure about your decision. It wrecks my teetering balance."

"Okay, I understand." He pauses. "I'm just trying to communicate that I might like to try having a relationship with you. It feels as if my life is missing."

"Thirty days," I say firmly, ignoring him. "Then we can talk."

Saturday, I have a full day with all the grandkids. Hannah and Orion come over, and we walk in the cemetery and play in the leaves. I watch as the kids run and climb trees. Beautiful fall colors, beautiful day, lots of giggles and snuggles. I feel great. For the first time in a while, at this moment, I am genuinely happy.

On Sunday, though, my stomach hurts. I wonder if I am only indulging myself—wanting a day off work—or if my body is inventing the pain.

I wonder if the ache is from cutting off Perry.

The pain gets worse. The next day, I drive myself to the urgent care center, where the doctor tells me my appendix has ruptured and I need emergency surgery. An ambulance is on the way. The nurse comes in with morphine. Stunned, I worry about health insurance and clients and appointments. The nurse tells me to relax. "Let us take care of you." The words make me cry.

Zac and Orion arrive, worried and solicitous. I am grateful they are such good men, but I wish they did not have to do this. I feel guilty for what I am putting them through.

The operation goes well. I am wheeled up to my room. The next day, shot full of meds, I make loopy phone calls and texts. Lots of calls come back, and the nurse's aide laughs at me. I am in high spirits. I am *alive*. I am high.

During my discharge, the doctor mentions that there appears to be a tiny cyst on my bladder that should be checked out. They've made an appointment with a primary care doctor in two weeks.

On my first day home, Perry calls to ask how I am. I must have morphine-texted him from the hospital. He said he thinks he wants to get back together.

Ricky is livid when I relay this conversation.

I say, "You know, when you trashed Dan after the divorce, it was great. I hated him. You hated him. But I don't feel that way with Perry. I know you worry that I'm holding on—"

"I don't think that," she says. "I just worry you'll waste time missing what he didn't give in the first place."

I understand her protective urge. Ricky thinks I would feel better if I realized I had so little to miss. But at the time, all I hear is what a fool I've been to love someone who turned out to be such a disaster

CHAPTER 33

Two weeks later, I go to meet my new primary care doctor. Dr. Smith is lanky and exuberant. He starts by saying I must have drunk from the fountain of youth. Good line. Very charming. He spends over an hour with me and then proceeds to order every test in the book. He asks permission to do an HIV test.

"Why?" I ask blankly. "I haven't slept with anyone but Perry."

He nods, waiting for me to get the implication.

It takes a few seconds. "Oh," I say. "Sure."

Perry may have left me, saying he was only *looking* for someone else, but clearly, this doctor thinks my husband was having an affair.

All those tests start me thinking about which organ will go next. Five years ago, in 2009, at fifty-six, I had surgery to remove what looked to be cancerous cysts in my pancreas. The prognosis wasn't good. I was opened stem to stern and lost my spleen and part of my pancreas. Thankfully, they didn't find any cancer. The following year, I again had severe pain. My gallbladder was removed. I've been fine since. But Dr. Smith tells me I came very close to dying with this ruptured appendix. I had no idea. Everyone had been so calm and matter-of-fact about it.

"The rest of your life is gravy," he says.

I leave wondering exactly what that expression means.

Zac and my grandson come over, and we go trick-or-treating. Our steep street is aglow with lit pumpkins and little trick-or-treaters. It seems a tradition on this street to sit outside with the porch light on, giving out treats and catching up with the neighbors. My grandson dances up and down the street wearing his skunk costume.

Perry calls over the weekend to see how I'm recovering. He talks about work and tells me he and Ann are over.

"I thought it was over before?"

He gets defensive and fudges. "Well, you asked if I was still in touch. But now it's really over."

"Wow," I say. "So you ended our marriage, caused us both to move, be financially broke, disrupted everything—and now you are not even with the person you took a sledgehammer to our life for?"

He goes on to say he shouldn't have abandoned our life; perhaps we could be close, romantic, and intimate again.

I try to focus on what I want rather than what might be happening in Perry's mind. Honestly, I'm not ready to walk away just yet. If Perry wants to give us another shot, I am willing, in a nod to fourteen years, to try. I want to understand what is or isn't possible with him—even if I worry it will be crushingly painful.

That evening, Ricky calls to ask me to the movies. I don't tell her about this most recent conversation with Perry because I imagine she'll be furious, not only at Perry but at me for even taking his call, for even considering this. We see *They Came Together* with Paul Rudd and Amy Poehler. It's a silly, sometimes laugh-out-loud spoof of the romantic comedy genre as the two of them imagine their relationship on the screen as a rom-com. Laughing with Ricky relaxes me and feels good.

On the drive home, I fantasize about what the trajectory of my own romantic comedy would be. It would start with a woman in her forties, just out of a difficult first marriage, learning to live on her own quite happily. She vacations with friends, her kids are thriving, she's learning about fun, but alas, no romance.

Then, in walks romance. No knight in shining armor, simply a really nice guy with a great smile who wines and dines her, is endearingly nervous. They kiss, and stars burst overhead.

They carry on an affair, but she hesitates at real commitment. After all, her newly independent life was hard-won. Finally, he wears her down with fun and sex and sweetness, and they get married and set up house.

She blossoms. From this new experience of being cherished, she ventures forth. Her career flourishes, her writing is published, her children do well, friends are supportive. She extols the amazement of love, the second-time-around kind, the-not-too-late kind. She's expansive and tries things she was hesitant to do before. Little things: she cooks, she cross-country skis, she paints watercolors, she writes. From this springboard of love, she has courage to take risks. This goes on for fourteen years, until one day, her second husband tells her he wants a divorce. He wants babies of his own, he states. He is no longer sexually attracted to her, he declares. And off he goes. The woman is seen devastated, drinking, smoking, and moping.

If this were a proper romantic comedy, eventually they would meet again by happenstance in a bookstore and go for coffee. After awkward and hesitant conversation, she would blurt out her belief that a love like theirs is too strong, too precious, too rare to give up on. A day later, he appears at her door. She opens said door in full makeup, dressed in casual-yet-sexy attire. He gives her a tentative smile, his eyes beseeching.

"I've been such a fool!" he says.

"Yes," says the woman, but doesn't invite him in. (We must give her some dignity.)

He's dressed in khakis and a blue polo shirt. They stare at each other with longing. He says, "I love you. May I come back?"

We end the movie there. Because in real life, there would be far too many questions, too much anger and recrimination.

But what if I changed the story a bit?

I can keep the premise. Older woman smart enough in many ways, not so smart in the ways of romance, falls for a man with an appetite for fun and frolic. He's kind and sexy, but without warning, he leaves her for a woman young enough to have babies.

If I make the story about the man lying and cheating (for some unknown amount of time) during their relationship, then the woman character is a fool to consider trying again.

If I make the story about the man having dementia and the woman character refusing to take him back, then she is the callous one.

If I make the story about the man being confused and scared of growing old, and the woman entertains the idea of reconciliation, then she is compassionate.

I need a goddamn story to hang the rest of my life on.

CHAPTER 34

A few days later, Dr. Smith calls to tell me I must see a urologist right away. He's made an appointment for next week. He is concerned I have bladder cancer.

It's a rainy and cold November day, but I bundle into my scarf and winter coat and go out on my back porch. It's become my favorite part of the house, set up high over the sloping land of my small backyard. Straight ahead is my back neighbor's house, and I can see beyond the roofs a few streets over. If I look to my right, all I see are the pines and hemlocks in the cemetery. I cry. I call Ricky and Nancy. I do not tell my kids. I also call Perry. It's been six months, and I'm reaching backward for the old comfort. Or, in my self-pitying state, I want to know if he still cares enough to worry. He picks up and truly listens. He says things like, if it turns out to be cancer, at least it was caught early, and assures me I'll be fine. I actually feel better.

Over the weekend, the grandkids visit, and we plant daffodil and day lily bulbs that will bloom next spring. It's wet, dirty work, and we slide around in the mud, giggling.

I'm in my study on Sunday evening, finishing up paperwork, when Perry texts about wanting to come down and asking if there is anything he can do. Immediately, I'm furious he is texting instead of calling. But a few moments later, he calls to ask if he should drive down. I hesitate. I tell him, no, I'll be fine.

I'm not ready to see him yet. If I let him physically comfort me around the terror of having cancer, if I lean into his arms and he pulls away again, I'll fall. And I'm afraid this time, I won't be able to get up. This phrase cracks me up, and I laugh out loud at my desk, straightening my back, thinking of the Life Alert commercial for old people: "I've fallen, and I can't get up." No, I have to face this one alone. I cannot risk another fall.

On the morning of my urologist appointment, I take care of the grandkids to distract myself. We finger paint and read books. Then it is time for me to go.

The nurse leads me straight into the exam room. There is no initial meeting with the doctor. She tells me to take off everything from the waist down and sit on the table. With my legs in stirrups and covered with a paper sheet, I wait a long time for the doctor. The room is small and filled with equipment I'm not familiar with. To my left is a small monitor and a machine with lots of tubing and something that resembles a wand.

The doctor is brusque when he arrives and barely says hello. "I'm going to do a cystoscopy and check your bladder. Ready?"

Ready for what? I think. Before I can ask, he inserts the wand into my urethra. There on the screen is my bladder.

"Yes. You have cancer. See?"

He points to what looks to me like colorful, wavy seagrass.

He removes his scope. "Get dressed and make an appointment with my nurse for surgery," he says, and walks out.

I stare at his retreating figure. This cannot be happening to me.

I get dressed, walk past the nurse, and straight out of the building. I will find another doctor.

I call Ricky immediately. We laugh—what is there to do but laugh? She promises she will find me another doctor. I will start over the process of medical procedures.

Perry texts: *How are you?*

I text back: *Cancer*

I call Nancy and Susan and let them know. We laugh some more. The absurdity of the situation is too much.

Perry calls to ask if there is anything he can do.

"Actually, there is one thing," I reply. "Tell me the truth of what happened."

"You're relentless," he mutters before he hangs up.

***

Over the next week, after Ricky finds me a new doctor, I schedule medical appointments. I get stuff organized. I read all I can online about bladder cancer. It is not comforting.

Perry calls on my drive home from Maine. "I worry I've caused you so much stress that I've given you cancer."

I laugh and say, "You don't have that much power." But it seems my cancer has become about his guilt.

As I continue my drive, I reflect that it was good to have appendicitis. Lucky even. This cancer was found early and can be dealt with. I will eat well and drink lots of water, and it won't recur. I work hard to stay in denial, but fear breaks through. Maybe it's a later stage. Maybe it's growing as I drive.

I switch to worrying frantically about financial loose ends: redoing my will and my 401(k) beneficiaries so everything goes to my kids instead of Perry. And what should I do about the kids? Should I tell them? When should I tell them? Maybe I won't tell them; they don't need extra worry. But I don't want to repeat what John did when he didn't tell his children he was dying. But I'm not dying, I decide.

I will tell the kids in three weeks over the Thanksgiving weekend when we are all together. I relax. I am doing okay, until get I home and there is an email from Perry.

Saying that things with Ann haven't worked out isn't

to say that I've necessarily given up on the idea of
being with someone new, or even on the desire to meet
someone else that I might have children with.

I imagine that he isn't even aware of how cruel he's being. But I do. Over the past month, he spoke of how he and Ann broke up, of his wanting to get back together, of not sure about continuing with the divorce, and now he's emailing that he still has the desire to meet someone new. Maybe my having cancer has made me a bad bet.

I don't respond to the email, and instead, I make a soup for dinner heavy on turmeric to boost my immune system and try reading a book.

My marriage crisis has been downgraded while I'm up against my cancer crisis. It's as if I have a red neon sign in my kitchen blinking: *Focus. Prioritize. Maximize your emotional resources.*

The next day, I call each of my children and tell them I have bladder cancer. I play it way down since I don't yet have clear information. All respond with concern and offers to help, but they do not panic. They are such grown-ups.

When I find out I have cancer, I believe it is a blip—a small hassle. This isn't just denial on my part. It is the ability to put scary monsters into boxes and pack them away in the basement.

This is a good skill for a child. As an adult, I have worked hard to learn how to unpack those boxes and face those monsters. I only keep one carton around for emergencies. Otherwise, when the electricity goes out, I might stumble around in the dark and trip over a box packed with horrors.

I decide cancer qualifies as an emergency. So, I put all my worries and fears and imaginings about terrible outcomes into the box and tape it shut. There is nothing I can do except show up for the surgery.

The boxes we carry around are filled with all kinds of hurts, real and imagined, from our childhood. As a grandmother, I tell my five-year-old grandson that hitting is not allowed in my house and stop him from striking his three-year-old cousin. "It is my job to keep you safe," I say. This is true. It is said calmly and with great love. This is a benefit of being a grandmother that wasn't as familiar when I was a mother. I am much calmer. I am willing to say things as many times as needed. I no longer expect toddlers, preschoolers, or teenagers to remember.

But what does five-year-old Forest hear when I say *stop*? What does three-year-old Sylvie hear when I tell her *no*? It rarely happens; I keep rules in my house to a minimum. But what is their experience? What do they feel? At three and five, do they already have cartons of scary monsters? Am I in one of those cartons they will have to unpack eventually?

My mother did not set out to silence me. She didn't intend to create a daughter who had to figure out how to be a person her mother wouldn't be angry at. My mother was trying to do all things right. After growing up impoverished with an alcoholic mom and married to a Sicilian where the rule of man was law, she was only trying to be a proper 1950s suburban mom.

But no matter my parents' intentions, I could not give voice to what I needed, what I wanted, or to ask when I needed help. I don't think the word *love* was used in my home growing up. I remember driving somewhere with my father and dropping off Zac, in fourth grade, at school. As Zac ran into the school with his backpack flapping, he called out, "'Bye, I love you."

My father was appalled. "He shouldn't do that. Scream 'I love you' across the schoolyard."

The world he'd grown up in was so very different. I imagine declarations of love could get you hurt on New York City playgrounds.

CHAPTER 35

Ricky finds me an acupuncturist to strengthen my immune system before the surgery. I also start reading *Anticancer: A New Way of Life*, recommended by one of my New Hampshire writer friends, which I find engrossing.

Just like that, I am reading again. Not exactly the kind of book I'd imagined sinking into, but no matter.

A few days before the surgery, I walk through downtown Boston in the pouring rain wearing my bright yellow slicker and funky yellow hat. I look like an advertisement for Gorton's Fish Fillets. As I watch everyone dripping by, I think some of these people are also going through tough times. Hopefully, they have figured out that handling it alone is not good.

The day before the surgery, I don't take care of the grandkids. In order to have my surgery, I must not be sick, and the kids all have some sort of bug.

I also feel slightly miserable. It is a completely free day, which is unusual for me, and although that should be a welcome prospect, I feel alone. And afraid.

I want to weep and wail. I want to rail at the universe! I have lost my sense of humor; my sense of future, my optimism, and my fortitude. My sense of myself. I don't want to be strong and positive all alone. I want someone to hold me. I want someone to tell me it's all going to be okay.

If I'm completely honest with myself, Perry is not this person.

A CD from Josh comes in the mail. It's Tig Notaro doing a

comedy set, along with a note saying, *I think you'll like this.*

I play it immediately. Tig Notaro starts with:

"Good evening. Hello. I have cancer. How are you? Hi, how are you? Is everybody having a good time? I have cancer."

In the audio, it's clear the audience is not sure if they should laugh or not.

She goes on to say, "It's weird because with humor, the equation is Tragedy plus Time equals Comedy. I am just at tragedy right now."

I start laughing. Her delivery is flat, matter-of-fact, and truly so funny.

She continues, saying that she was hospitalized with a severe bacterial infection; a week later, her mother died in a freak fall; then her girlfriend left her; and she was diagnosed with stage II cancer in both breasts. All within four months.

"But," she says, "you know, what's nice about all of this is that you can always rest assured that God never gives you more than you can handle. I just keep picturing God going, 'You know what? I think she can take a little more.'"

I laugh and immediately fall in love with her. I play it again and laugh some more.

CHAPTER 36

On the day of my operation, Zac drives me to the hospital. It is an outpatient surgery. After we hug goodbye, I am led away. I go from station to station as they check me in, take my clothes, take my vitals, and hook up IVs. First is intake, then pre-op, then the operating room, then the recovery room, then finally discharge. At each stop, I am asked, "Are you alone?"

"Yes."

"Someone will take you home?"

"Yes. My son is coming to get me as soon as he is called."

The next station.

"You are alone?"

"Yes."

"Do you have help when you get home?"

"I live alone." I sigh. "If I need help, like someone sleeping in my house, please let me know now."

"No, no. But someone will check on you?"

"Yes."

The next station.

"You are here all alone?"

I have dear friends who all offered to drive, to stay, to pick up, to take care. I also have great kids who do drive, pick up, and take care.

What I don't have is a partner.

They need to find a better way to check on a patient's status.

The surgery goes well, and the prognosis is good. The doctor tells me to think of it as having a skin cancer removed. "You are lucky it was found so early. It was barely there. Just keep going back for checkups, and we'll remove anything if the cancer returns."

No chemo. No radiation.

The doctor is helping me play my game of *it could be worse*. I could be ninety-one and have buried all my children. I could be a young mother with cancer, not sure she'll see her children grow up.

I might not know what happened to my marriage, but I know some things. I know that how I think impacts how I feel, which in turn affects how I act. I talk a lot about this in the groups I run.

If I think *I have gotten a raw deal* or *I am too old to start again*, I feel angry, defeated, and depressed. I walked hunched over and weary.

If I think, *What is wrong with me that I cannot maintain committed love?*, I feel deficient, afraid, and hesitant to be with anyone.

If I think *Life is a fucking wild ride, and I am grateful for the love that I have been given and am still being given*, I feel expansive, and I smile and walk straight.

If I think *Life is full of change, embrace it*, I feel excited and energized, and make plans to plant bulbs and take classes at the arboretum.

In other words, while I don't have control over my circumstances, I do have control over my reactions.

The cancer diagnosis forces me to acknowledge in a concrete way that life is finite. It removes all illusion that I have time to dither and distract myself about how I want my life to go someday. It obliges me to come to terms with what I have, what I want, and what I believe is essential right now. I do not recommend waiting until you are diagnosed with a potentially terminal disease to reach this understanding. However, it is useful if it is given to you.

Just like that, I feel like I am waking from a bad dream. Gone is the abandoned, old, alone, financially strapped, weeping woman. In her place is a woman filled with purpose and determination. I am fucking grateful to be alive. I want to finish my new novel. I want to see my grandchildren into adulthood. I want to travel to Venice. I want to be as healthy and strong as my age allows.

I make the most awful healthy smoothie ever with spinach and nut butter—but it will be okay. I can drink it. I still have heartache. It's like a stomachache, only worse. It's right around my solar plexus. I can feel my face scrunch up, my lips quiver, and my eyes fill. I hold my breath. I remember to breathe.

I do miss *old* Perry, the one I knew in our marriage. I don't miss *new* Perry, who has gotten stranger and stranger since he left, someone who complains at length without asking anything about me.

No matter what Ricky thinks or my kids think, this is not the man I was married to and loved for all those years.

The man I was married to had a tendency toward self-obsession. Who doesn't, especially when stressed? But usually, we have enough social graces to say *Hi, how are you?* before we launch into rants about how the cable company screwed us over. And if we do launch into a tirade, we usually have enough of those graces to apologize to the person on the receiving end. That's all gone from Perry. It's weird, and I return to my dementia theory. I search the internet, find the Mayo Clinic site to remind me, and here we have it.

> *In frontotemporal dementia, parts of these lobes shrink, known as atrophy. Symptoms depend on which part of the brain is affected. Some people with frontotemporal dementia have changes in their personalities. They become socially inappropriate and*

*may be impulsive or emotionally indifferent. Others
lose the ability to properly use language.*

I focus on the behavior changes. These include:

*Increasingly inappropriate social behavior
Loss of empathy and other interpersonal skills, such
as having sensitivity to another's feelings
Lack of judgment
Loss of inhibition
Lack of interest (apathy), which can be mistaken for
depression*

I skip over the behaviors that don't seem to apply:

*Repetitive, compulsive behavior, such as tapping,
clapping or smacking lips
A decline in personal hygiene
Changes in eating habits, usually overeating or devel-
oping a preference for sweets and carbohydrates
Eating inedible objects
Compulsively wanting to put things in the mouth*

I have no idea if this is an accurate diagnosis; however, the
frontal lobe dementia theory allows me to focus on just missing
the relationship and not on what was wrong with me.

In our marriage we didn't bicker or snap or make digs. We were
kind to each other. We did not criticize. We cuddled and rubbed
each other's feet.

Come on, there are always issues, a voice in my head insists.

Okay. He loved to play. I also loved to play, but he loved to play
more. Sometimes, I also like to clean the house, weed the garden,
and organize the garage. I think this made him feel guilty as he

read in his chair.

Sometimes, he wished I didn't work so much. Now and then, I wished he worked more. I frequently wished he would see more of a connection between money coming in and money going out. I was more practical: the recycling needs to go out, the checkbook must be balanced, and my reports should be finished. He was more: let's do it tomorrow.

I wished he was more able to relax around my kids and enjoy the chaotic and loud family gatherings and outings. He tried, but it wasn't easy. With such a large extended family, we have a lot of gatherings and celebrations. So, Perry and I accommodated this reality: I went off to see family without him, giving him a pass, except for the major events. But it did make me sad not to share such an important part of my life with him, especially as grandchildren came.

But none of these "issues" would have prompted me to even think about leaving. If he hadn't left, it simply would have been that the rocks in my head matched the holes in his.

The frontal lobe dementia theory doesn't change anything, but it gives me a rest from self-blame and softens my anger. It frees me to concentrate on staying healthy and paying attention to what's in my life now. A diagnosis of frontal lobe dementia often can't be confirmed until a brain autopsy is done, so I won't ever know.

There is no cure, but if my diagnosis is correct, it will be slow.

***

Life is a series of moments, and sharing those moments is what gives them meaning. I will miss sharing life moments with Perry. He brought out the playful in me. The lighter side. The part that could leave chores undone, walk by the ocean, and then read the Sunday *Times* over breakfast by the water. The part that could order room service and otherwise be irresponsible.

The part that could say, yes, let's go out to dinner, to a movie, to Hawaii.

I have a hard inner taskmaster. I have lists to get through, money to earn, books to write, dirt to clean, gardens to weed, emails to return, calls to make, exercises to do.

But I can relax that inner taskmaster. I can choose to do that. I can be responsible for my own joy. I can choose to live life moments with people who love me.

***

For the month of January, I cling to my frontal lobe dementia theory. It is a leaky life raft, but it does its job. With this theory, I don't have to reevaluate every memory. I don't have to feel rejected and experience all the less-than self-judgments that have been unearthed.

That would be like feeling rejected by a partner with Alzheimer's who can't recognize you anymore. How silly would that be?

I know this is a bit nuts. But I decide it is harmless nuttiness. It allows me to feel compassion for both of us. I decide denial-in-stages is the way to go.

As often as our schedules allow, I meet Ricky for a walk in the Forest Hills Cemetery first thing in the morning. Big hats, puffy coats, scarves wrapped so that the minimum amount of skin is exposed, we walk the paths circling the pond. Ricky listens patiently. Even though she thinks I am delusional, she is tolerant of my need to hold onto some theory that excuses Perry from being a jerk and me from failure at understanding anything.

***

Last week, my writers' group met up for drinks and dinner in Portsmouth. A mother described the pain of watching her nineteen-year-old son deal with a breakup. "She told him she was 'too busy' to have a relationship," the mother said. Then she asked her son, "What is that telling you? What do you think that means?" The son answered, "She has an anxiety disorder." The mother held her head in disbelief and said, "He thinks she'll come back to him."

I think Perry has frontal lobe dementia, and I'm sixty-one, not nineteen. My friends hold their heads in disbelief.

I want to say to that nineteen-year-old: I know how hard it is to let go. Letting go means our love wasn't all that we believed. It means we had no clue what was really going on with our lover. It means we have a flawed understanding of reality.

Maya Angelou wrote, "Surviving is important, but thriving is elegant."

I might not know a lot, but I know this: I intend to thrive—elegantly.

CHAPTER 37

At the end of January, seven months after he left, Perry informs me that he has decided to take time off to travel to Vietnam and see Ann. Obviously, they are back together. I am relieved. He will be halfway around the world. Not calling or texting and throwing me off balance. Perhaps I can thrive more elegantly this way.

I make spinach and berry smoothies and start consuming copious amounts of turmeric to keep cancer away. I concentrate on making a life.

I continue to travel back and forth to Maine. I make dates with friends. I write up a schedule. I find time for writing, walking, people time, playtime, massage, weights, work, and grandchildren. I'm trying to put order into my days.

Before Perry left our marriage, I felt young, energetic, and full of plans for the future.

Then he left, and I got old.

The negative messaging about what it means to be old is pervasive and has been worrying me since I turned twenty-five. I worry about growing stupid and not knowing my children's names, or having strangers clean my body, or no longer being able to move because my hip hurts so badly, or being unable to afford strawberries, or falling asleep before the end of the story. For me, aging has always meant loss and grief. I wonder if I can learn to treat aging as an adventure. If I can lean into my fears of aging and dying and grapple with them? Like most people, I fantasize about going out gracefully, but I'm not even sure what that means. I've been with many as they died. But to create a mindset of adventure—this feels exciting.

My youth will return. I can feel that now. Especially since I have quit smoking and drinking and am eating an anticancer diet. Well, obviously I won't regain my youth exactly, but I won't feel so ancient. I can feel the tide turning—slowly and like sludge, but turning nevertheless. I am wondering what I will do next.

Ricky takes me for a makeover at Bloomingdale's; Greg invites me out for dinner; and Susan asks me to see the musicians, Dwight and Nicole, play at the Lizard Lounge in Cambridge. Another life is germinating.

My two-year-old granddaughter arrives for a playdate. We sit on the floor, playing with cars and tiny zoo animals.

"I need my sippy cup."

I say, only half in jest, "I'm not sure how to get up."

"Like this," she says. And she demonstrates by putting her two hands on the floor and her ass in the air and pushing.

I laugh so hard, I fall over.

I am sixty-one, and it is clear that my body does not work as it once did. I am still young enough to be surprised. I expect that twenty years from now it will no longer be shocking. I expect that I will have developed strategies and techniques to move off a floor, to begin the process of locomotion that is familiar to two-year-olds, who are learning to run and jump.

What I decide to do is not let embarrassment get in my way. I am determined to still get on the floor and play with cars that are traveling through mazes of wooden blocks. Even if it means that I need to put my ass in the air to get up and get the sippy cup.

***

And then the snow comes. This winter is the snowiest winter on record in Boston. With no place to put the snow, the streets become narrower and narrower. Walking is treacherous, driving is slick, and the T often doesn't run.

I sideswipe a neighbor's car, taking off both of our mirrors. Swearing loudly, I put a note on his car. I call the repair shop and discover it will cost in the three-hundred-dollar range for each car.

The car owner calls to say thank you for being honest and not to worry. We will be in touch.

His voice is low and sexy. Wouldn't that be a great, classic ending to my romantic comedy? The woman meets the man who will become her friend, lover, and companion by hitting his car.

In between blizzards, I manage to meet my friend Greg for dinner. He agrees to go to Venice with me. He generously behaves as if my frontal-lobe-dementia theory is something to seriously consider. I have fun and feel almost normal.

It's going to be okay. I will be okay, maybe even downright good. I will go to Venice. I will have close relationships with my grandkids. I will write novels and read great books. I will get in shape. I catch glimpses of myself as a whole, happy person: my brain buzzing, my muscles strong, my lungs expanded, and my heart laughing. I am beginning again. I am grateful I have the chance to begin again. All is good.

I believe there is nothing left to throw me off-kilter.

***

I see an old friend from high school for the first time in ten years. Mitch and I had a falling out. He and my friend Judy were part of the commune days. He is also the director of the domestic violence program I worked in previously when I lived in Boston. In addition, he is an outrageous flirt. During our lunch, he flirts with me shamelessly as we travel over many topics and years, reconnecting. I wish I hadn't banished him for so long.

That same evening, at my grandson's birthday party, I see my ex, Dan. I mention that I had lunch with Mitch. Dan asks me, "What caused the falling out?"

I say, "To be honest, I don't even remember now."

Dan laughs. "When will you say that about us?"

"Never. I have all the journals from those years in the basement."

I am pulling back into my life people whom I have loved and cared for. I am sending out threads and beginning to weave a new life.

***

As I walk down the snowy streets and strangers say hi or smile at me, I think, *Ha! They're noticing an attractive, energetic, engaged older woman.*

I realize I still carry around with me the self-image of a graceful, pretty woman. I'm shocked when I look at pictures. Old, lumbering, gray-haired with nice smile is more accurate.

I've always photographed badly, I tell myself. I decide not to look at the pictures.

I am choosing to live with these two delusions that I photograph terribly, and strangers say hi because they admire me. There are worse ones I could choose. I could choose to live with the delusion that I control the world, or should, so I'm always upset when things don't go the way I plan. I could believe that at sixty-one, the world owes me something, and feel pissed when it doesn't come my way. I could insist that aging and dying are not in my cards and be horrified at the process. I could choose to live with all sorts of delusions that would cause me to be upset, angry, resentful, and scared.

Instead, I choose to feel graceful and believe that strangers on the street are wishing me well.

If necessary, I will change my terminology. Instead of getting old, I will become an elder. This sounds much more dignified and worthier of respect.

***

I try to limit my whining to my computer. In my journal, I sometimes circle back to believing that I should have forced Perry into therapy or said no to the divorce. I should not have called him weeping and drunk during those first months. Maybe when he said how much he missed me and our life together, I should have said, Come back. Was it lack of courage on my part? Not wanting to face all the messy, anguished work of repairing a relationship? Did I only want the easy? Maybe I should have let him win at Scrabble.

WHAT???? my journal yells back at me.

He was like a dog with a bone, actually a man with a boner, one that hadn't popped up without Viagra in recent years. He'd found his fountain of youth, and he was going after it with a single-minded pursuit he actually failed to employ in the rest of his life.

With Ann, he feels young again, sexy again, powerful again. He imagines adventures and babies. He has no idea what having a newborn and raising children entails. But it certainly will distract him from worrying about aging and death. His life will be filled with drama and challenges, and this may work for him for the rest of the days he has left.

And for you? You will put down your roots. You will feel solid ground under your feet. Now, go write and do your work!

So, I do.

CHAPTER 38

It's been nine months since Perry left, and Valentine's Day is coming. Self-pity flares. Perry was always great with this holiday. He bought sappy love cards that I cherished, small gifts like my favorite cookie dough ice cream, and always flowers. So, to celebrate singles awareness day/friendship day/quirky alone day, I buy a bunch of tulips and an extravagant tropical flower bouquet for myself. I love these new names.

Later, Ricky takes me out for my sixty-second birthday. We walk on paths tunneled through the snow, slipping down the hill. Boston is expected to get another sixteen inches in a few days.

The day before Valentine's Day, I wake up to an email from Perry.

> *Gin,*
> *I thought knowing the itinerary of my trip to*
> *Vietnam might help;*
> *I'm going to be catching a 2:30 am bus to the airport*
> *in a little while. Will be in touch.*

I stare at the flight information. Why would he think my knowing his itinerary to Vietnam would help? Help what? Help who?

It's like picking a scab. Yep, still hurts like hell! Okay, just checking.

But before I can think about this, I become violently ill with a stomach flu. Coincidence? There are many different ways to purge.

***

With Perry, I felt like my boat had a deep keel and could sail anywhere. I was excited about new adventures.

Now, my boat feels very tippy. That deep keel crashed on some unseen rocks and shoals, and I got bounced around. The sail is tattered, the rudder loose. Although I was rescued and pulled to shore, the damage to the boat was great, and it will take time to repair and get back on the water. Although I did not suffer lasting physical damage in the wreck, I was walking around asking, *How could I have navigated so poorly, not known about the hidden shoals, been so careless?*

I was following the map Perry had given me. Could he have given me a wrong map? On purpose?

It's that question, of course, that rattles my brain.

My journal yells at me again.

GET THE FUCK ANGRY.

I don't want to be bitter and angry and nasty.

Fine. So, don't get stuck in it. But you still have to feel it.

I don't want to be angry, bitter Gin. I don't want to end up like my mother.

BINGO. I was wondering if you'd ever get there.

***

My kids and grandkids tromp through the snow for a visit. The weight of my grandchildren curled against my body as I read story after story is a pleasure indescribable. I would have liked this pleasure to be purely a bonus in my life, not a solace. But we don't always get to choose.

***

In March, I extend my stay in Portsmouth for a few extra days before Sally's inn starts getting busy for the season. I plan to catch up with writer friends, take long walks along the Piscataqua River, check in with the publisher, and work on revising my new novel.

At the end of a long writing day, I take myself and my notebook out for oysters at a restaurant overlooking the harbor. I will watch the sunset.

I notice an attractive couple, sixtyish, being seated across from me. She is slim, wearing a white cabled turtleneck sweater, her blond hair pulled back in a ponytail. He's got a full head of thick gray hair and has only an olive-green wool shirt on as a jacket. They discuss which side of the table to sit for the best view. She chooses, and he slides in next to her. I imagine they're dating. But as he orders fried scallops, she wonders out loud if that was a good dinner choice for him. Married, I decide. He touches the nape of her neck, and she stiffens. Yep. Definitely married.

I go back to writing and slurping oysters that taste like I'm swallowing the essence of the sea. My phone buzzes.

It's an email from Perry saying he's back from Vietnam and there is a problem with the paperwork for the State of New Hampshire retirement system, and so we have to redo it and sign it again.

I sigh and look up. It's the paperwork of life that can kill you.

Now, the couple is switching sides because the sun is in her eyes. He taps her shoulders, her neck, the top of her head. At each tap, she flinches and finally tells him to stop.

His mouth sets, and he turns away. Her mouth sets, and she stares straight ahead.

I go back to my oysters and Perry's email. He writes that he has a lot to talk to me about, but he isn't ready. He is very confused about what he wants, and he misses me. He has decided not to move to Vietnam. He thinks he'll be ready to talk soon. I turn my phone off.

I look up when I hear the man complaining to the waitress about not having bread yet. I hear the waitress explain that the bread burned. "So sorry," she adds.

"Do you know how often I hear that?" the man asks.

The waitress is young and not sure how to respond. "I'll bring the bread as soon as it's ready," she says.

"Get the manager." The man waves her away.

She leaves, face flushed. The woman stares in the other direction, out the window.

The manager, her dark hair twisted in a bun, dressed in black pants and a white top, comes to the table. "I apologize," she says. "The bread burned."

"Why?" he demands.

"The chef made a mistake." I am awed at her patience.

"It's been almost thirty minutes. Why did he burn it?"

She keeps apologizing. The man won't be placated.

I want to go over to the table and tell him to stop being an asshole, and then perhaps his wife could endure his touch. I want to tell the woman to pay attention to what she's feeling. She's not doing anyone any favors, least of all herself, if she can't stand the man.

I would so rather be alone.

In the fading light, I walk carefully on the brick sidewalk, slick from the melting snow, back to Sally's inn.

CHAPTER 39

Later that week, I am sitting outside on my back porch. Although there is still snow climbing up the back fence, the March air is warm and soft.

Hannah, my daughter-in-law, calls to tell me she is pregnant. I am ecstatic with the news of a new grandchild. We talk for a long while. I'm still smiling when the phone rings again. It's Perry.

"I need to tell you something," he says.

I wait. The birds, excited by the spring air, are loudly singing their mating songs.

"I didn't go to see Ann this visit to Vietnam," he says. "I went to see someone else."

He's got my attention now.

"I went to see Binh."

I'm confused. "You're dating random Vietnamese women now?"

"No."

Binh. The name floats back to me. This is the student intern who arranged for him to teach in Vietnam in the first place, right before he left me.

After Binh finished her studies in the United States and returned to Vietnam, Perry helped her with curriculum planning for her teaching. When I was reading or working, he'd occasionally say he was going downstairs to Skype with Binh and talk about her teaching.

"I don't know why I lied and told you I was seeing Ann on this trip," he says.

Cold distance eclipses all other emotions. "Why ever lie to me? Especially now, after we are *already* divorced?"

"I feel a bit nuts," he confesses. "My life is out of control. I got it into my head somehow that I needed to do things before I died, like have hot sex and a baby."

I watch the birds swoop across the yard. Does he not know how misplaced, not to mention hurtful and disrespectful, it is to tell me these thoughts? He sounds feverish, even a bit manic. But I am not the person to help him.

"Are you seeing a therapist?" I ask yet again.

"I wish I didn't put in for retirement," he continues, oblivious. "I realize all the things I love to do—reading history, beach walking, and all the rest—are in the context of our relationship."

"You need to see someone," I insist. Overpowering sadness floods through me when we hang up. He doesn't sound well at all.

***

Perry and I meet in Portsmouth a week after that phone call, on my way home from Maine, to sign what I fervently hope will be the last remnant of the divorce paperwork. This is the document that will allow the State of New Hampshire to deduct the portion of his pension due me and cut me a check.

Back this past summer, when he first left, when we were negotiating this issue with the mediator, Perry balked at paying half of the $500 filing fee this would cost. He suggested that he'd send me the $300 each month.

"No," I said.

"Why?"

"Because I don't trust you."

"You don't trust me?" he asked, shocked and wounded.

I laughed.

Now, we are at Book & Bar, a new café and bookstore in the old Custom House. Small tables are surrounded by shelves and shelves of used books for sale. People sit sipping coffee and speaking in hushed tones as if in a library. Perry and I talk a little about this and that. I tell him about Hannah's pregnancy. He tells me about arranging to continue teaching after his retirement. It is both a comfortable, easy exchange and totally bizarre. We have entered into an Escher painting, where the everyday is identifiable yet completely distorted. We sign the papers. He walks me to my car.

We hug goodbye. I get in my car and futz for a minute, making sure my phone and water bottle are within reach. When I look up, he is still there, leaning against the nearby brick building, staring at me and sobbing. Great, gulping sobs. People on the sidewalk step around him, then look back and hesitate, wondering if they should do something.

I roll down the window. "What's going on?" I ask.

"We should be going home together," he calls out. "I love you. You should not be driving off."

I also start to cry. I don't want to, but I can't stop. My face twists as I try to suck the crying back.

He doesn't step away from the building. I don't get out of my car. "But you wanted this," I say. I am completely undone as I drive away. His weeping on the street is heartrending, and proof that the man I loved is falling apart.

He's sounded so bizarre these past ten months. Shouldn't I have noticed this crazy earlier, somewhere in those fourteen years? Round and round, I go. The repetitive nature of this dynamic is wearisome. The outcome is always the same. Gin's personal movie version of *Groundhog Day*.

CHAPTER 40

We have only sporadic contact over the next month. Now, when I read through my journal and I see *Perry called*, I think: *Don't pick up. Don't pick up.* I turn the page. *Damn. I picked up.*

During the week, I am still traveling back and forth to Maine for work, a sixteen-hour day, because staying at Sally's in Portsmouth is not an option during her busy season. I now also have work in the Boston area. Once a week, I travel to Brockton for twelve hours. I work from home on other days. I have my private practice. I write. I plant my garden, see friends, and take care of the grandkids. My life is full.

Almost a year to the day after Perry left, I am sitting on the back porch fantasizing about the garden I will plant. It's a warm May afternoon. Tulips poke through the remaining patches of snow-slush in the garden.

Perry calls. "I'm in the hospital with a severe bladder infection and sepsis from an enlarged prostate," he announces even before saying hello.

"That sounds awful," I say. I have a twinge of anxiety. Sepsis can be life-threatening. He tells me he will leave the hospital with a catheter and urine bag strapped to his leg. He will need this until he decides on what treatment to use to shrink his prostate.

Over the next couple of days, there are texts from Perry about urine bags, Flomax, and peeing. You fool, I think. This is one reason people don't leave caring and loving relationships at sixty. No one wants to be alone, old, and frightened in a hospital. I text back kind things. *How awful. Hope you feel better soon.*

This is the kind of stuff wives must deal with. Not ex-wives. Still, he's scared. I call him. I ask about Binh. He tells me she's frustrated to be so far away. After listening to more urine bag stories, I beg off the phone.

I wonder why I'm hearing these stories. Maybe he hoped I would rush to help him. Of course, the larger question might be why I'm listening. The thing is, I still care, even if part of me thinks I shouldn't, even if my friends think I shouldn't. I do. I opt to forgive myself for this.

The next afternoon, after a day with the grandkids, I sit again in my favorite spot on my back porch, played out, enjoying the warmth.

I always feel quite successful at the end of the day when the grandchildren are all alive and minimally damaged.

I consider if it is healthy for me to be so satisfied with these little people's love, then I have an image of Perry bumbling through his day with his catheter, dragging his urine bags around, and decide I have traded up.

I close my eyes. The birds and squirrels are loud and busy—it's gratifying to be in the middle of the city and surrounded by birdsong. I resolve to someday identify all the birds by their songs. The spring sun is strong, and in one day, all the tiny patches of snow have finally left the garden.

Ricky emails, asking if I want to go out for dinner on Saturday. I respond yes and then see a series of emails from Perry.

There are things I've been holding back.

There's more? I look away from my screen. The blue jays are attacking the squirrel climbing my neighbor's feeder. I watch them for a bit and move to the next email.

212

*There never was an Ann. I made her up. It has been
Binh all along.*

I'm confused. I read the next one.

*Binh and I were married in Danang, three months
ago, this past February, on my most recent trip to
Vietnam.*

I don't understand. Perry is married? I sit back and try to
absorb this. I notice the blue jays have retreated in silence. The
squirrels have conquered the bird feeder.

Since leaving, Perry has doled out information about this
woman named Ann to me, drop by drop.

Now he tells me Ann doesn't exist.

He described their airport meeting, gave her a college friend,
chose her a graduate school, and even created a dinner scene with
her mother and brother on his last night in Vietnam. He made her
up, an entire woman? He fabricated her like I do with a character
for a book?

And meanwhile, three months ago, he married Binh, his former student?

I reread his message a number of times. I forward his email
to everyone who has been listening and caring for me. Then I call
him.

When he picks up, I start right in. "Why didn't you tell me?
Why didn't you tell me *after* we were divorced, at least? Why all
the weeping? Why all the emails about how wonderful our life
together was, how you missed me, all those moments you said you
wanted to come back?"

I'm yelling, still on the back porch. My voice startles the
birds, who are screeching again at the squirrels at the bird feeder.

Everyone in the surrounding houses can hear me. I don't care.

"Why, *after you were already married to someone else*, were you crying on a street corner, talking about how we should be going home together? Why did you make me listen to your urine-bag stories? How could you have put me through this for an entire year *after* you'd already left?"

"I had doubts."

"What?"

"People have doubts after they get divorced and remarry."

I hang up and send him an email.

> *And what about Binh? Does your new wife know about your weeping and your "doubts"? I've always described you as such a kind, loving, smart, sexy man. But none of those words are valid. You are simply a selfish old man who can't pee.*

Zac comes over and sits with me on the back porch. "Well, that's that," he says, and reaches for the wine bottle to top off my glass.

***

Over the next week, as I travel to work, play with my grandchildren, wash dishes, and plant my garden, my mind tangles with questions.

In the early morning hours, when I finally give up trying to sleep, I marathon-watch the Netflix show *Grace and Frankie*. It's about two women whose seventy-something husbands, who are law partners and friends, leave their wives to be with each other. The men had been having an affair for twenty years and hid this from their wives.

I find this show comforting in an odd sort of way. It means

other people have relationship drama into their sixties and seventies. The two women are devastated and not coping well. I also find this comforting. I'm not that unique in my grief.

Grace, played by Jane Fonda, asks Frankie, played by Lily Tomlin, "Why aren't you angry? He ruined your life. He humiliated you. He abandoned you in your last years. Why aren't you angry about that?"

Frankie says, "He just didn't know how to do it."

I like this line. It doesn't mean Perry's a scumbag, or an evil man, or never loved me, or any other number of things that I choose not to believe. It means he wanted to leave and didn't know how to do it.

This feeling of generosity won't last. The anger will surge again, then recede, then surge again. But I'm glad to have felt it. *He just didn't know how to do it.*

It prompts me to send Perry a text:

> *Hurt and heartbreak flood my world right now. But I do wish you peace.*

He responds a little later:

> *I wish you the same.*

And there it is! Fifteen years. From start to finish.

CHAPTER 41

As soon as the weekend arrives, I go into a cleaning and organizing frenzy while my mind and emotions whirl. How far back does his relationship with Binh go? Ricky and I start calculating. If they first met when she was a student intern, that would be in 2009. She visited our house and came for dinner. At the time, she was engaged to someone she met in her graduate program. After her internship, she planned to return to Vietnam and then come back to the States on an engagement visa. As far as I knew, she'd been gone for years. Did it begin that summer? That would mean it was a five-year affair. I don't like this. I want it to be a much smaller amount of time. I want my memory of our happy life to be true for longer.

While living with Perry, my narrative was one of a happy second marriage with a kind and gentle man. Then it changed to a happy second marriage that ended abruptly because Perry wanted babies. Then it changed, yet again, to a questionably happy marriage that ended because Perry had met a young woman on a trip. My narrative had to be constantly amended over these past months because he kept changing the goddamn story.

***

The stories we tell ourselves about ourselves are powerful. Our sense of self is formed on narrative, the continuing stories regarding our lives—who we are, where we came from, and where we are going.

When Perry first left, my immediate story was about being

unlovable. Fundamentally unlovable. It was an ancient tale rooted in childhood, and I was stunned by its force as it spewed from the depths, an erupting and fiery volcano of self-doubt, self-loathing, and shame. Lava and ash threatened to bury all I was, all the love given me, and all who I loved.

Luckily, there was another small part of me that wondered if perhaps, just maybe, this story was inaccurate, not to mention a bit crazy. Plus, I was surrounded by people who loved me, held me, and supported me. For this past year, my struggle has been digging through all that ash and molten rock to come up with a story about why Perry left, but that did not mean I was unlovable at the core.

I tried desperately to find a story that would preserve my narrative of a happy-in-love marriage while also explaining his leaving. That was less possible. I strained to find a theory that would explain his leaving that would protect my belief that he was a kind and good man. Also, difficult.

Now, my narrative has to change all over again because he keeps altering what happened.

Hours into my cleaning outburst, I'm buried deep in the pantry, excavating ancient cans of pinto beans and tuna. I scrub shelves and read expiration dates. Now, it's a story of Perry having a long-term affair while I was clueless. Now, I understand. I just have to deal with what a zillion others have dealt with. I loved a man who had a secret life, and I never knew it. This feels both supremely uncomfortable and uncomfortably familiar.

Perry planned a marriage and a wedding to Binh while we sat holding hands in front of the fire in our wood stove.

My father laughed and drank cocktails with my mother and neighbors while visiting his other family twice a week.

My brother John mowed the lawn, played with his young family, and worked long hours while having clandestine involvement with men.

I wonder how people manage such double lives. How do they keep track of it all? I can barely get done all the things I need to do in one life. Lists litter my house: birthday reminders, friend dates, garden chores, work obligations. How do you do two?

As I fill a trash bag with half-finished bags of limp potato chips and stale cereal, I think about our trip to Italy a few months before Perry left. I remember drinking espresso and eating gelato in Rome. I remember holding hands as we walked through ancient olive groves, the trees twisted with time. I remember sitting in the garden of our rented house in Pienza, surrounded by lemon trees, while Perry cooked pasta and mushrooms upstairs. We were so comfortable together and took so much joy in each other as we went on our adventure through Italy.

But now I realize that while on that trip, he was choosing between me and Binh. It changes the memory. It changes me into a fool and him into a con.

I slump into a chair. I'm surrounded by half-empty shelves and expired cans of tomato sauce. I have no interest in finishing this job. I leave it all a mess and make myself hot tea with sugar, which always seems to help in British novels, and take my mug to my spot on the back porch.

Perry emails me yet again.

> *I think about you often and what a good life we had together.*

I write him back:

> *We didn't have a good life together. We had a good lie together.*

I'm pleased with my cleverness.

But I don't send it.

***

Everyone lies. Everyone dissembles, has pretenses, hides things. Everyone engages in self-deception. Even as a therapist, I have major blind spots. I try my damnedest not to, but it is difficult. I sandpaper a bit of my split wood, paint my veneer, and pretend—even to myself—that the cracks aren't there.

I don't feel well, I may say when I need a day in bed to read. This is not a major transgression. But it's there. I'm probably being self-deceptive as I write this. There are probably bigger ones.

Looking back, I think about how easily Perry lied. He would say yes to things like dinner with his sister, but at the last minute, he would make up some story to get out of it. My father used to call this "telling a little white lie." A way to keep social interactions smooth. Like my father, I want to believe these are harmless, but I'm not so sure anymore. Perhaps small lies to protect people's feelings lead to bigger ones that end in betrayal.

I also know what it is like to have secret selves. In high school, I was the good girl, the honor student, always respectful. Then on the weekends, I smoked dope, dropped LSD, and slept with Dan as we made plans to run away and change the world.

Years later, I dye my hair to cover the gray and wear makeup to distract from the wrinkles. I hid my smoking addiction for years.

Now, I hide the true extent of my desolation. In front of clients, my bosses, and my grandchildren, I crack jokes and show a lot of teeth when I smile. I am fine. I do not reveal how I watch the clock, desperate to get to a corner where I can weep as if my broken heart will never heal.

I try to present to the world what I hope is the best version of myself.

Of course, presenting my best self to the world is different from having a secret life. But perhaps it's different only in degrees.

I work with people who lie very well. I have learned that I really can't tell who's lying from who's telling the truth. It's humbling. I'd like to believe I can spot the difference.

I also recognize that as I hang out with my adult children, I tell different stories to each of them. I don't mean different versions, although I'm sure that's true as well. I mean, one son might hear of my car breaking down and my adventure with the tow truck driver. Another son hears about what a friend at work said to me about our boss, and another hears about the amaryllis blooming. There is no reason for this. It's only what is on my mind at each moment. But the stories we tell create views of us—and my children will all have different ones of me.

Yet, it isn't as if one particular view of me is more genuine than another.

My brother John loved his wife and children. He was an accomplished and talented man. He also loved men. This was not a part, a version of himself, that he believed he could share, for whatever reasons.

My father fell in love with another woman. He waited over ten years, until I started college, before leaving his marriage because he wasn't a man who abandoned his family.

And Perry? I believe at some point he fell in love with a young woman who wanted babies. I believe this opened up a path, a possibility that he had thought he was too old to pursue. I do not believe that Perry wanted to put one over on me. I believe he was torn. We did have a good life together. He just wasn't sure what to do.

"Yes," a friend agrees patiently when I tell her this. "That could be accurate. But why couldn't he involve you in this decision that impacted you both so greatly, as opposed to glibly inform you?"

I do wish Perry had handled everything differently. I wish that he had been able to come to me and talk about his struggles with aging, his worries about dying without children or about me dying and leaving him, and his attraction to a young woman. But he isn't a person who delves deeply into his psyche, asking questions like: *Why am I acting on this attraction to another woman? Why am I jeopardizing my marriage? Do I want out of the marriage? Why? Perhaps I should get help.*

This is backwash thinking, of course. Who knows what I would have done if he had talked with me about this? He was in a conundrum. The person he usually talked things out with was me, and he knew if he started expressing his doubts about our marriage, my distress and fear would confuse him. He did not want to encounter my hurt. He chose avoidance over honesty.

And me? Why was I content to live with a man who didn't do such intense self-examination? Maybe so that I could fill in the blanks for him. Because I didn't see him wrestle with doubt, I took that absence to mean he didn't have any. I could project onto our relationship all those feelings of romance, sexiness, fun, and caring and assume this was all true. I was grateful for the ease of our togetherness after the constant clashes in my first marriage. He was my safe space, my conflict-free zone, my curl-on-the-couch-and-feel-held home. I forgot that the absence of visible conflict doesn't mean its actual absence.

And during our years together, I was very engaged with my kids. Even grown kids come with their share of drama, and a large part of my brain was frequently occupied with hoping they didn't careen down a path it would be difficult to recover from.

But for Perry? What was it like for Perry? Was it boring to feel like a "safe" space?

We only get one life. Should Perry, based on some moral code of goodness, have refrained from going after what he wanted? Really, should he have? Or my brother? Or my father? I wouldn't want Perry, or any of them, to wake up and realize at the end that they'd lived someone else's life.

CHAPTER 42

In our sixties, if we're lucky, we're starting what Anne Lamott calls the third third. Although I don't have a specific terminal illness, I am aware that my life is limited. Not in the sense that I could get hit by a bus tomorrow (really, how likely is that?), but in the sense that I have more past than future.

When Perry and I were both approaching our sixtieth birthdays, I began talking about death. I'm not obsessed; I'm practical. I wanted to complete our wills. I wanted to fill out our medical proxy forms. I wanted to know if he preferred to be buried or cremated. Did he want all lifesaving measures or not to be resuscitated? I wanted to take care of this, so if, God forbid, I did get hit by that bus tomorrow, I wouldn't spend my last moments alive thinking, *Shit, I never got around to filling out those forms.*

Perry did not want to talk about getting old and dying. He did not want to choose between burial or cremation. He did not want to think about it. Even though every single person who has ever lived on this earth has died, I think it felt like a personal affront to him.

I get that. I even feel that.

We are experiencing this aging thing for the first time, and doing anything for the first time is difficult, clumsy, and makes us feel scared and inadequate.

I only wanted to take care of the paperwork so I could go back to believing that I would live forever, while, as it turns out, Perry was deciding he wanted to have children.

There is no right way to age. Some of us are overwhelmed with the grief of lost youth. Some are exercising their way to eternal life. Some are taking risks, jumping out of airplanes or out of jobs, risks they were too scared to do when younger. Many are engaged with the medical system. Some are despondent with regrets. Some, like me, are in joyful denial.

Turning sixty, as the artist Ann Pruitt says, can create an edginess, a desire to upend your life, make a dramatic change to avoid the dread of whatever is coming next. Not me. I was content, grateful even, to be facing with Perry anything old age would bring.

But I think Perry faced sixty with dread, and he imagined his fear could be managed by leaving me and the life we'd made and tumbling into a new life with a young woman. Creating a new beginning possibly allowed him to believe it would postpone his ending. He could fill his life with busyness and distraction. Or perhaps my aging body, my brush with cancer, came too close to watching his mom with Parkinson's and his previous partner die of breast cancer. He didn't want to usher anyone else out. Choosing someone much younger would be a good hedge against that.

In the beginning, after Perry left, I kept asking myself the same question: Who leaves at this stage? Sixty is the age of leaving the house only to return for car keys; the age of, Have you seen my glasses? The age of sudden, unwanted diagnoses. Who leaves a marriage at this point?

Turns out, a lot of people.

The divorce rate for people in the U.S. fifty and older is now almost double what it was in the 1990s. There is even a name for me: *silver splitters*.

Ugh.

I learned I was not alone. But starting over on my own in my last third wasn't how I had anticipated spending my sixties. I'd imagined me and Perry together till the end, laughing and commiserating as we handled the shifts and tweaks aging requires.

CHAPTER 43

Recently, I've joked that the sum total of my wisdom is: we're all a bit nutty. I mean this only in the kindest way. At times, we all delude ourselves, harbor distortions, envy others, deny reality, suffer paranoia and anxiety, crave love, feel out of control of our emotions or our behaviors. And this is only the short list.

Along with our boxes of monsters, all of us have pockets of crazy. When I act from my pockets, I damage people I love, including myself. I say mean things, withdraw, have another glass of wine, buy a pack of cigarettes.

I do think it's a good idea to reflect upon our unique pockets of crazy and the particular boxes of monsters we lug around. (I am a therapist, after all.) We can't always change those pockets of crazy, but we can learn to notice them and be gentle with ourselves. Sometimes, we can even alter how we cope and identify who we might be hurting when in a delusional space. We can learn how to spot when we're heading in that direction.

But it takes a great deal of effort and time, of willingness and understanding, to examine our own pockets of crazy. It goes against the convention that there are normal people and there are "other people."

I like believing all of us are a bit crazy. It helps me feel acceptance for myself and other humans. It helps me connect and be less judgmental, less sanctimonious, and less certain that I know the right path for anyone else.

Thinking all of this through helps me remember that Perry is not an amoral con man. He is a sixty-year-old man with unexamined pockets of crazy.

***

A few days after Perry tells me he's married, Zac and the kids come over for an early morning visit. I ask Zac to arrange for Perry's emails to get forwarded to another email address so they won't come into my inbox at all. It is past time. I no longer want to be jolted out of my current moments by random missives from Perry.

I think about the famous line from Mary Oliver's poem: *What is it you plan to do with your one wild and precious life?*

It is a question I want to consider in earnest.

First, I tell Ricky that I am going to let my hair go gray. She does not think this is a great idea but sends me pictures of different hairstyles with gray hair.

I've decided to do it not only because it would save a great deal of money, but because I am no longer interested in pretending to look younger than I am. I want to enthusiastically claim every year I've lived.

Then I plan a trip with Ricky to Provincetown, Massachusetts. Two weeks. We will walk, eat lobster, and write.

Provincetown, on the very eastern tip of Cape Cod, is a magical place, part old fishing village, part art colony, part gay and lesbian mecca. The ocean, the air, the sun are just what I need.

I used to subscribe to the as-soon-as method of living. As soon as the baby is born or off to college, or I finish that project at work, or winter is over, then I will create world peace, end hunger, plant roses.

While in Provincetown, staring at the ocean, watching the waves tumble, listening to the screech of seagulls, I decide on the wave method. Relax your body when the waves you never see coming tumble you, dive into them when you do see them, and swim like hell during the lulls in the breakers.

***

Of course, I still want to know things about Perry. I want to know exactly when he decided his dream of Binh was worth pursuing. I want to know if during our times together, when I felt the sweetness and the pleasure of a deep and abiding love, he was itchy, wanting to be away.

I want to know if my version of our story was anything like his version of our story.

But I have to learn to live with not knowing. I have to be comfortable with not knowing.

Just as I do not know how John got AIDS or the specific demons Ken and my mother fought with alcohol or why my father had another family.

I'm not saying it wouldn't be gratifying to have more information about these people so I could sort through it all, mull it over, and reach an *Aha* moment, a moment when the puzzle pieces all fit together, where the dots are all connected.

It seems that humans are always searching for answers to the mysteries of the cosmos or the mind. We want to know, to fathom the depths. But sometimes, it's not possible. People contain multitudes as vast as the stars.

At the time, learning about the secrets and lies of my father, John, and Perry felt like a betrayal of the relationships I thought we'd had. I was indignant. I thought you were *this* kind of person and you turned out to be *that* kind of person.

But maybe the people I love are not responsible for the fact that I thought they were one way and later found out they were another way. None of these people set out to betray me. They were merely managing their crazy pockets the best way they knew how.

CHAPTER 44

When I left Dan at thirty-nine, my father said how brave I was to leave my husband when I had three children to care for. Such courage.

It wasn't courage. It was basic survival.

When I met Perry and decided to risk loving again, *that* was courage.

I remember vacationing with my friend Greg in Provincetown. Perry and I had known each other a few months by then. As I was waiting for Greg to pick me up and drive us to the Cape, Perry called. "I love you," he said.

I spent that next week on a deck in Provincetown, watching the boats on the bay and writing that it was okay to take a risk. All love is a gamble.

I was scared.

At that time, at forty-seven, I understood that love and attachment were risky undertakings. John had died at forty-three, and Ken was dying. Both my parents had died. Judy, my closest friend from childhood, had died the previous year.

My father left my mother after thirty-two years of marriage.

I left my marriage after we'd been together for twenty-four years.

Each person you love takes a piece of you, and then they are careless, forget to look both ways, drink too much, climb mountain cliffs, or are otherwise negligent.

People die. They fall out of love. They leave. We grieve these losses.

My grandmother lost her first four children before her fifth, my aunt Mary, survived. Later, she lost another child.

The only way to avoid this heart pain is to avoid love. And that is too hard a way to live.

A familiar childhood game I remember playing is "Would you rather?"

Would you rather lose your sight or your hearing? Your arms or your legs?

Seniors worry about losing their independence or their minds.

Loss is a constant and yet such a huge fear. We protect against it. We install smoke detectors and immunize our children. We try to be careful with money. We move to safer neighborhoods and don't curse out our boss.

So, when loss comes anyway, we blame.

Even when my three-year-old grandson loses his lovies and is bereft and panicky, I want to say, *Keep track of these important things and you won't feel so bad.*

I don't say it. Instead, I say, "I know they can't walk out by themselves, so I promise you we will find them." And we usually do.

We judge. Why wasn't I more careful? Why did you walk on that street in that neighborhood? Why didn't you get out earlier when you knew war was coming?

These judgments are not evil. They are simply our human attempt to believe that if we do all things right, we will be immune from devastating loss.

I took the risk. And I lost.

Am I sad that I lost? Oh, most definitely.

Am I glad I took the risk? Yes.

Years later, I can say: Perry's leaving did not diminish the parts of myself that his loving unleashed. That person still exists in the world. And I am grateful for that.

CHAPTER 45

Three years later, my youngest son, Josh, is engaged. He and his fiancée, Meirah, are visiting in Boston.

In the morning, Meirah is curled on the couch, and we are drinking coffee in our pajamas. She has long hair that waves down her back. She is talking about how much she loves Josh, what a wonderful man he is, and how lucky she feels.

"At what point ... did things go wrong with Dan?" she asks me.

I know she is asking for reassurance that their love will last. Or for some glimpse of how to recognize when the relationship might be faltering.

"I don't think things were ever right with Dan," I say. "But I was too young to really understand that."

"But what about Perry?"

"That was a different story." I shrug. I wish I had some nugget of insight to offer. Love gone wrong is an outrage that is painful to experience and painful to watch. We want assurance that it won't happen to us, that it won't happen to those we love, that there are signs to watch for, portents, spells to weave. And perhaps there are. I don't happen to know any of them, or I would happily pass them along.

***

Six months later, Josh and Meirah are getting married in the backyard of a neighbor's house in New York State, near where Meirah grew up. Both the wedding ceremony and the reception are intended to be outdoors. It is a lush setting filled with flower gardens, fountains, and greenery. Plan B, in case of rain, is to move it all inside, but it will be very cramped and have no room for dancing. There really isn't a workable or good plan B.

That morning, the sky is ominous, and clouds roll in. The rain starts. The weather forecast calls for the rain to end by four in the afternoon. The ceremony is scheduled to start at five.

Three of us watch as the rain falls in sheets. It doesn't appear to be letting up. There is lots of anxious conversation about when and if to move the whole thing indoors. I suggest they wait a bit longer.

Meirah leaves to get dressed. Josh and I watch the puddles form on the rented folding chairs set up on the lawn.

"So, Mom," he says, "do you still believe in love and marriage?"

I want to take my time here. Josh has witnessed me go through two divorces. He, along with his brothers and my niece and nephews, gave loving, funny toasts at my second wedding about how pleased they were that Perry had come into all of our lives.

"Yes," I say carefully, "I do. It didn't work out for me, but I still think exploring and getting to know a person till the end of days is a superb and worthwhile endeavor." I pause and say, "Love alone is not enough. You need to be fearless."

The rain ends exactly at four. The catering staff towel-dry the chairs. The day goes beautifully. Not perfectly. But beautifully.

CHAPTER 46

People around me are beginning to ask, Are you seeing anyone? Are you dating? Are you having sex? This last question is implied rather than directly asked. (The answers are no, no, not telling.)

I understand their motivation. It is some version of getting back on the horse.

A happy ending for this saga of lost love would involve me meeting another love. It isn't a terrible notion. I am a sucker for love. I am still the woman who watches romantic comedies. I am still a believer.

Friends and family members would relax if I fell in love again. They would stop imagining long, bleak, lonely evenings for me. Probably the only people who wouldn't care if I was in a relationship or not are my grandchildren. I love them for it.

Because a funny thing happened during my grief over Perry—I discovered I really like living alone.

It's difficult to describe being alone and happy without sounding like I'm trying to convince myself that low-fat yogurt tastes as delicious as ice cream.

I wake in the predawn hours and am able to follow my thoughts down convoluted paths without interruption. I read late into the night and then wake up a few hours later and read some more. I spread pages of my book in progress over the living room floor and stare at them, moving a chapter here, switching a chapter there, until my eyes get blurry. Then I leave it all and move into the garden to dig holes, letting my brain clear. When I return to the room, I play music, turn Aretha Franklin up loud, and rearrange the pages again. I leave it all when I have to go to work. It disturbs no one. I eat cereal for dinner and cook chicken and cauliflower for breakfast.

Of course, although I live alone, I am rarely alone. I invite grandchildren for sleepovers, friends for dinner, and family for walks. Ultimately, Perry was right. I *have* nurtured a wonderful community of family and friends.

I get glimmers that I've been given a gift.

I read a book once in which a young woman is having trouble getting pregnant and is very sad about it, and an older woman tells her: "If the Lord sets you free, be free indeed."

I decide that could apply to husbands. Even the best, most loving husbands require a lot of caretaking.

I was trained early as a caretaker. Whether it's because of the era I was raised in; or because in childhood, I saw my job as helping my mother not lose her mind; or perhaps because of my temperament, it's difficult for me *not* to be a caretaker. But I grew up less skilled in knowing how to care for my own emotional needs. I tend toward numbing behaviors, like smoking cigarettes and drinking another glass of wine or keeping overly busy.

So, after Perry left, after I made it through the shock of it all, I became a better caretaker of myself. It has been a journey of discovery. Of skill building. I learned to ask for help and be gracious in accepting it. Taking care of myself means resting when tired, encouraging outside time, not creating daily to-do lists that actually require three days to complete, and feeling proud when I accomplish what I am scared to do.

I learned to understand that I cannot create happiness for anyone else. I can share joy and wonder, I can crack jokes, join in laughter, but I cannot create a sense of serenity in another person.

I can encourage and cheer them on, I can soothe hurt and troubled feelings, but finding a sense of well-being is their own work to do. That is an inside job.

And, of course, that applies to me. My happiness cannot rest on another person.

I also understand that I can't prevent suffering. Not even for my children or grandchildren or friends or clients. I can sit with them. I can advocate for them and help them find resources. I can hold their hands. I can offer a shoulder to cry on and stand beside them, but I can't prevent suffering. And I no longer believe I can.

I found this statement from Maria Robinson profound: *Nobody can go back and start a new beginning, but anyone can start today and make a new ending.* I appreciated that I am not beginning again, not starting over. I am creating a different ending.

And with that altered perception, whole worlds of understanding open.

I no longer believe that I am a failure at love. I have lifelong relationships and strong friendships with family and friends. Turns out, I have long-lasting loves. Just not long-lasting husbands.

I let go of the idea that I need to make a great splash, solve the world's problems, or devote myself to saving the earth. I recycle, but I really have no idea how to protect endangered species or get the world to pay attention to climate change. Or end poverty. Or child abuse. Or racism or other inequities. I have opinions about these things, but really, I have no idea.

I've become humble.

I know a few things. I can be kind. I can be generous with my time and with what resources I have. I can listen to people in pain so they know they are not alone. I can smile broadly with genuine appreciation when my loves of all ages say, "Watch this! See me!"

I savor small pleasures. Daffodils and cardinals. Growing beans we can eat. With my grandchildren, I travel to Pluto and Saturn. I pull my novel out of the drawer and dust it off. At work, I ask for a raise and get it. I focus on birdsong in the predawn light.

I still believe in love. But part of my romantic notion was having someone to share this getting-old thing with, someone who also was growing old and who knew me and loved me before I was old. Obviously, there are never any guarantees for this kind of future, but I still find the idea sweet and poignant.

I appreciate the way long-lasting couples love, the private jokes, the shorthand, knowing each other's rhythms, the look across a room of people that says, *I've got you.*

What I have instead—what I have created—is a life of connection with love. Not *a* love. Not *one* person. But a life of love nonetheless.

There is a freedom of being in my sixties and exhilaration in being mistress of my own life.

So many books end with finding the right person. I want to end luxuriating in finding me.

EPILOGUE

Five years later

I am retiring from my full-time job, and this is my last day. I am giddy. For the first time in my life, I will be completely free to choose to do what I want, when I want. It is the sensation of being let out of school for the summer. Anything is possible. I feel healthy and vibrant. I am about to go off on a two-week writing retreat in Provincetown. I am thrilled.

My phone buzzes. It's Perry. We haven't talked in a long time.

"Hi?" I say, my voice lifting into a question.

"Do you remember, after I left, that you wished triplets on me?" he asks.

"Yes."

"Well, your wish sort of came true. Binh and I just learned that we are expecting identical twin boys."

I burst out laughing. I can't help it. Karma.

"Congratulations," I croak out. "How do you feel?"

Naturally, Perry expresses worry. He vents his concerns. He feels overwhelmed. Some things never change.

"You will be a wonderful father. You know how to appear loving, caring, and calm, no matter what turmoil is roiling inside you."

I am not entirely sure if Perry feels the sting of my words. I suspect he is too distracted. He will be a first-time father at sixty-six, and I sense this reality is only beginning to dawn on him.

I hope he has good life insurance.

We've certainly chosen very different paths to live out the rest of our days.

***

When I'm back from my writing retreat, I meet Perry for lunch. We eat lobster rolls in Portsmouth as the sun glints off the water, watching the gulls follow the tugboats on the Piscataqua River. It is May, and his tennis tan has begun. His hair, like mine, is mostly gray, as is his mustache. His shirt collar is frayed. Definitely time for that favorite to be retired, but I can imagine how soft it would be to touch after so many washings. From across the table, I can smell the slight hint of lavender laundry soap. He looks tired. It is nearing the end of the school year, and I'm sure he is worn out.

He tells me I look wonderful, and I smile my thanks.

The waiter clears our plates.

"Do you remember," I ask him, "that before you left, I told you the next book I intended to write was about the gifts of later-in-life love?"

He nods, tearing up.

"I still plan to write that book," I tell him. "Only now it has a different ending."

ACKNOWLEDGMENTS

So many people, over so much time, helped me write, complete, and publish this book. I am so grateful for everyone I've loved and learned from.

My family offered immeasurable support, encouragement, and love during the events that prompted this memoir and the actual writing of the book. My sons, Orion Kriegman, Isaac Kriegman, and Joshua Kriegman; my daughters-in-love, Cynthia Kriegman and Meirah Kriegman; and my niece, Kirsten DeLuca, and my nephew, Todd DeLuca, patiently engaged with long and repeated conversations about the meaning of love and life and reminded me about radical self-acceptance. My grandchildren, Darwin Parker Kriegman, Brighid Stella Thomas Kriegman, Forest Maitri Kriegman, Sylvie Celeste Thomas Kriegman, Oakley Solomon Kriegman, Luca Galanti Kriegman, and Hazel Cherry Kriegman, brought me joy and giggles and awe, which eased all difficulties. My grandnephews John Joseph DeLuca, Leif Cyrus DeLuca Gould, and Heyward DeLuca joined the love fest by calling me Nonna. Victor Gould's steadfast creation of his music showed me the importance of persistence. Louise Romagoux, my sister-in-law, gave generously of scrubbing and being excited to read whatever I wrote. I am indebted to Kevin DeLuca, Scott DeLuca, Shawn DeLuca, Mia De Franco, Isabella DeLuca, Sydney DeLuca, Cole DeLuca, Mike DeLuca, Silas DeLuca, Julie DeLuca, Haidee DeLuca, and Hannah Thomas, for being an integral part of my family web and history.

My women's group, Diane Butkus, Randy Susan Meyers, and Susan Powers Knight, has consistently been the backbone of my life. They have always encouraged my writing and given me endless love. Cyrisse Jaffee, Nancy Wilson, and Mitch Rothenberg shared stories and offered strong love, much-needed feedback and editing.

I give great thanks to Randy Susan Meyers, my forever friend and brilliant writer, who first suggested that I write a memoir.

Thank you to my writing community, and especially to Alysia Abbott, an extraordinary writer, and teacher, head of Boston's GrubStreet Memoir Incubator program, who, besides teaching many necessary aspects of craft, offered feedback that had me reaching into my depths. Alysia also created an ongoing community of writers that kept me steady as COVID began and the initial draft was completed. I am beyond grateful to my fellow members of the Memoir Incubator class of 2020—Rita Chang, Ann Crane, Linda Cutting, Ani Gijka, Karen Kirsten, Theresa Okokon, Trần Vũ Thu-Hằng, and Anri Wheeler—for reading multiple drafts and uncovering a book among an incoherent mess of pages. Kristen Ng read generously and founded Title Doc, which helped me find my title. Thank you to my larger writing community, which generously shared their time and praise: Ada Calhoun, Orna Guralnik, Sarah Ruhl, Maya Lang Shanbhag, Margaret Sofio, and Abigail Thomas. Thank you to Meirah Kriegman, who designed my website and offered endless patience while I was dealing with my tech challenges. Thank you to Jovielle Gers, the photographer, who made taking my picture a pleasure. I greatly appreciate Susan Shapiro, a phenomenal teacher who helped me learn how to pitch essays, and thanks to Noah Michelson, editor of HuffPo Personals, who said yes to my first national publication. I'm indebted to Nancy MacDonald and Elizabeth Barrett, extraordinarily skilled editors who kept improving the manuscript. I am so grateful to Ann-Marie

Nieves from GetRed PR, and Elina Vaysbeyn, publicity and marketing gurus, helping to get the book to readers.

Thanks to my agent, Helen Zimmerman, who never gave up submitting the manuscript and kept me believing in the book.

I greatly appreciate Apprentice House Press and the Loyola University community working to create this book: Kevin Atkins, Director; Molly Gerard, Managing editor; Niki Ignacio, Design editor; Maggie O'Donnell, Promotions editor; Aspen Shelton, Development editor; Sophia Strocko, Acquisition editor. Thank you to you all.

About the Author

Virginia Deluca is a writer and psychotherapist. She is the author of the award winning novel, *As If Women Mattered*. Her essays have appeared in the *Iowa Review*, *The Writer*, and *The Huffington Post*. She lives and works in Boston, Massachusetts.

Apprentice
House Press
Loyola University Maryland

Apprentice House is the country's only campus-based, student-staffed book publishing company. Directed by professors and industry professionals, it is a nonprofit activity of the Communication Department at Loyola University Maryland.

Using state-of-the-art technology and an experiential learning model of education, Apprentice House publishes books in untraditional ways. This dual responsibility as publishers and educators creates an unprecedented collaborative environment among faculty and students, while teaching tomorrow's editors, designers, and marketers.

Eclectic and provocative, Apprentice House titles intend to entertain as well as spark dialogue on a variety of topics. Financial contributions to sustain the press's work are welcomed. Contributions are tax deductible to the fullest extent allowed by the IRS.

To learn more about Apprentice House books or to obtain submission guidelines, please visit www.apprenticehouse.com.

Apprentice House Press
Communication Department
Loyola University Maryland
4501 N. Charles Street
Baltimore, MD 21210
Ph: 410-617-5265
info@apprenticehouse.com • www.apprenticehouse.com

www.ingramcontent.com/pod-product-compliance
Lightning Source LLC
Chambersburg PA
CBHW052212240425
25704CB00024B/473